SEND ME WHERE NO ONE WANTS TO GO

God's Assignment
Into the Darkness of Africa

The Carole Ward Story

BY

BARBARA H. MARTIN

Send Me Where No One Wants to Go

Copyright © 2017 Favor International, Inc.
All rights reserved.
ISBN
13:978-1975711511
10:1975711513

Cover design by
Katherine E. Busbee
Technical Assistance by Charles R. Thibos
Headshot of Carole by JC Penney
Barbara's Picture on Back Cover by
Jessica Forinash

Scripture is taken from
Zondervan NIV Study Bile

Most names have been changed. No parts of this book may be reproduced, transmitted, downloaded, decompiled, reverse engineered, or stored in or introduced into any information storage and retrieval system, in any form or by any means, whether electronic or mechanical – except in the case of brief quotations in articles or reviews - without the express written permission of
Favor International, Inc.

CAROLE WARD
Founder/Director of
Favor of God Ministry, Uganda
and
Favour Africa Ministry, South Sudan and Favor
International, Inc., USA

Forward by the Author

While my name is on the front page, much of the writing has been taken from newsletters by Carole Ward in order to retain the flavor of the way she speaks, thinks and feels about this ministry. The result is a dramatic account of what God has done through her Ministry.

It has been an honor to tell about the miracles, signs and wonders of a living God who used a "mere" woman to accomplish His will. I use that word because that is how women are still perceived in Africa to this day. The Lord gave Carole the zeal, energy and fearless determination to carry His Word into the darkest corners of the world when she asked to be sent where no one wants to go. In return for her obedience and perseverance, He then backed up His Word with signs, wonders and miracles, just as He did in the book of Acts.

I hope I succeeded in sharing them through Carole's eyes and with the personal feelings of her heart.

Although this is not a book about Carole Ward, but about the great love, power and divine intervention of a mighty God who sent His Son to die for a people in a world of never-ending wars and destruction. It is a tale of redemption, deliverance and triumph against all odds of a living Savior called Jesus Christ, who defeated the enemy of darkness, witchcraft and unspeakable horrors with His power and love for a people forgotten by the world.

Come, join Carol on a journey into the dramatic world of a modern-day book of Acts and be blessed beyond measure.

A Village in Uganda

Chapter 1

The Night of Fire

Burning mud huts after an attack by LRA rebels

The rapid gunfire outside was followed by piercing screams. I sat up with a jolt. It was in the middle of the night and my heart was pounding as I jumped out of bed and rushed to the window. In the eerie light of the moon I could see nothing but the outlines of mud huts along the dirt road. Their straw roofs looked like giant hats in the darkness. Just as I turned to step back, my eyes caught flickers of flames light up the night. In seconds, several huts were burning and people ran screaming from the inferno, which minutes ago, was their home.

Fear gripped me like a vice and for a moment I had trouble breathing. I fell on my knees and began to weep for this land.

"How can I stop this, Lord? How can I overcome the godlessness, the witchcraft and endless cruelty in this country called Uganda? I am only one woman. What can I do to overcome the spirit of hopelessness, poverty and fear in the town called Gulu where anarchy, murder and hate are the norm? But most of all, how can I understand and have compassion on a people I don't know and have no idea what their lives have been like for the last eighteen years?" I was crying now, not from fear, but from frustration and helplessness. "How can I possibly feel what they feel unless I live with them, Lord? How can I live with them if I am afraid to face what they face every day?" I was trembling as God's answer came clearly.

"Give them Bibles instead of bullets."

I suddenly felt calm. God had spoken. I was not alone. He was with me and would accomplish what no man could do – bring His love to a people the world had forgotten. Was this not what I had asked for, to go where no one else wants to go?

The heat from the burning houses all around me was stifling and the continued shrieking outside pierced my soul and I cried out again, "How can I stop this horror and godlessness, Lord? How can I, one lone woman, come against the powerful spirit of witchcraft in this place, the hopelessness and devastation? Lord, I didn't think it would be this terrible. Without Your help, there is no way I can make a difference, but with it, I can do all things, like Your Word says. The screams outside intensified as I continued to pray, sobbing uncontrollably. It was hard for me to concentrate with the horrible turmoil outside my house, trying not to allow fear to take over my heart.

"You have sent me, Lord. Give me the power to overcome Satan and his demon forces. You know I don't have what it takes, but I do believe Your Word which says You have given me authority over Satan and his forces in the Name of Jesus."

"Did God really say?" The voice of the enemy whispered in my mind. "You can't stop the bullets or my power, because you are alone. This is my land and I control it. Go home like all the others before you."

I rose up from my knees and stood, suddenly filled with a sense of power that was not mine.

"Satan and your demons, get away from me in Jesus Name," I said out loud. "You will not hinder or harm me because Jesus defeated you on the cross and has given me authority over you."

The voice of the Lord was unmistakable, "I will never leave you nor forsake you. You are my servant and My Spirit will go before you and nothing whatsoever shall harm you."

"Show me what to do, Lord," I asked.

"What would you do if you couldn't see your hand in front of your face?" God was speaking to my heart.

"I would look for a light, Lord."

"Light dispels darkness as truth dispels deception. My Word is light. Take it like candles across the North and darkness will flee." I sat very still as His Word penetrated my spirit. It became the motto for our ministry, "Move God in and everything else has to move out."

The turmoil in my heart suddenly faded away as I lay down on my narrow, wooden bed and closed my eyes. God would find a way.

My thoughts went back to how it all began so many years ago.

The Lord's harvest fields had been part of my life since before I was born. My maternal grandparents were missionaries in China for 30 years and my mother was born there. When the Communists invaded Shanghai, my grandparents and their children were taken to a prison camp. They were later released as exchange prisoners of war.

In 1960, my parents went to the fields of the Philippine jungle and served the Lord for 48 years as missionaries, as well as Bible translators for sixty years. Growing up as a missionary child in the Philippines helped shape the longing of my heart to help the poor, the oppressed, the widows and orphans and those who are victims of war and suffering. It was during this time, a burden to reach those who had never heard the Name of Jesus started in my heart. After all, why should millions know about Him in churches and on TV in my country, when even more millions all over the world had never had the chance to hear about Him even once? This became the driving force in me from then on to take

Jesus where no one had gone before. It has never left me to this day.

I came back to the United States as a teenager, received my nursing degree, was married at 17, and began therapeutic foster parenting for emotionally disturbed and traumatized children. I continued with that ministry for the next twenty years, in addition to raising my own 3 precious daughters. At the same time, I worked as a nurse in home health and hospital settings, and eventually opened a nursing center for Alzheimer's patients. I served in my home church as administrative staff for several years in the capacities of leadership training, evangelism, discipleship and citywide prayer ministries.

In 2002, I had a chance to go to Kampala, the capital city of Uganda for a three-week mission trip. It left me dissatisfied. What good can anyone do in three weeks? I began to feel a growing desire in my heart to serve the Lord in this country, not just for three weeks, but for the rest of my life, and go to a place where no one wanted to go. It was as if God branded my heart in the shape of this war-torn, battered nation.

During my second trip, I met a seventy-year old missionary with Campus Crusade. He was a remarkable man, who had grown up with the Pygmy tribes in the deep jungle of Congo and had given most of his life to serve the Lord in Africa. As I listened to his fascinating stories of how his missionary grandfather used to hunt elephants with President Roosevelt and other amazing missionary experiences, I was even more sure I was supposed to serve the Lord in areas where Jesus had not been preached. Yet, once again, I knew in my heart it was not this particular area the Lord had for me, because someone had already established a ministry there.

After I returned to the States, I continued to weep in prayer over the unreached people in Uganda. The Lord showed me they were part of His bride who didn't know she was His bride.

"I will call them my people who are not my people; and I will call her 'my loved one' who is not my loved one," and "It will happen that in the very place where it was said to them, 'You are

not my people,' they will be called sons of the living God."
Romans 9:25-26

Not long after, I got a letter from Kampala in which the white-haired missionary asked me to run his mission called Lake Victoria Christian Center, a two-year Bible school in Kampala. It sat on 80 acres and was made up of 60 full time teachers and staff from five East African countries.

Since I strongly felt this was not my final place of ministry, I wrote him back, "You don't even know me."

His return answer was short and simple. "Yes, I do."

It took me five months to pray about it until I finally agreed to go for one year. I had no money or any idea what to expect since deep down in my heart I knew this was not the final place the Lord had for me. When I arrived, the old man showed me around the camp and was gone the next day! And so, my training as a long-term missionary had begun. This is where I learned the basic principles and patterns of raising up nationals to eventually take over the work for the time the old missionary, or any of us, would eventually leave.

Upon returning at the end of 2003, he named me principal of Lake Victoria Christian Center. The school had a 14- month intensive Bible training school and was situated on an 80-acre campus in Kampala in the South of Uganda. It also had the oversight of 42 portable Bible schools in five east African countries.

One hundred and sixty students were enrolled from four east African countries. They were receiving strong Biblical instruction through 40 different courses that were designed to equip them for ministry as pastors, youth leaders, children's workers, evangelists, teachers and church planters in rural villages.

Greater than any administrative duties related to the campus was the yearning in my heart to see the Holy Spirit poured out upon these hungry students in a mighty way. As I spoke in chapel services, prayed with staff and students and joined them for times of worship and intensive prayer, I was knit with them in the Spirit as we cried out for revival in their tribes and the many ethnic groups in the area. Our greatest desire was to see God use each of them to reach their own people with the powerful message of the gospel.

The longer I was there, the more I realized, if this ministry was to survive until Jesus comes, it was vital the local Christians be taught to stand strong without missionaries because the missionaries would eventually leave. I went to work creating an infrastructure by training local leaders to run a medical clinic and other outreach work for their people. I wrote a field manual for coordinators for five surrounding countries to help others reproduce the work without the help of the white man. I traveled to 42 bush Bible schools and taught them about farming, managing money and other vital subjects they needed to know in order to organize and run their own ministries. It soon became evident the Lord had sent me to Kampala to train me to train others and establish His Kingdom to prosper without the presence of outsiders. He impressed me that if I go into one village, He will be there, but if I train one hundred to go, soon He will be everywhere.

"What village do You want me to go to, Lord?" I asked one night in prayer.

"Can you believe Me to do it right now on this campus and seek revival to bring down My Glory?" His Holy Spirit filled my soul as I held my breath and then said, "I want to put my face into the dirt and travail for revival to come, Lord." At that moment, I felt His anointing come over me as I cried out on my knees, "Send me, Lord. I believe."

The next day, I announced all classes would be stopped and declared three days of fasting and prayer for the entire school with a twenty-four-hour prayer chain undergirding our meetings. These were students from different denominations and countries who came together, united with one goal, to bring down the Glory of God. The results were miraculous as the first day brought repentance, the second ignited revival and the third established restoration which totally transformed 150 students from Uganda, Kenya, Congo, Rwanda and Sudan, who would take God's message to their nation just as the Lord had showed me. Yet in spite of it, there was a struggle in my heart. *This is not the place I am supposed to be, Lord. Someone is already here. I know I am supposed to go where no one else wants to go. Please, show me.*

During that year, the Lord did remarkable things with the ministry. Once a month, I invited pastors and their wives for a meal and taught them about the Kingdom of God, leadership training and character development with a special focus on the sustainability of God's vision, dependent on character and without outside help. These were great weaknesses in most African countries.

Our outreach expanded rapidly across the area and even to the north into Gulu District. It was here where my heart knew I was supposed to be.

As the horror stories about the wars in the north reached us through many of our students who made it to our Mission, seeking help, I felt theirs was like the Macedonian cry and cried with them to the Lord every night to the point my pillow was wet with tears.

"Send me, so Your love can bring light into this horrible darkness. I know I am only one woman, but You are a big God and I don't need anything but Your anointing to change this nation." **"I can do all things through Christ Jesus who strengthens me." Philippians 4:13 (NKJV)**

One day, when I traveled with African team members on a four-hour journey northward, the Spirit of God began to move on our hearts as we traveled in the car. When we crossed the Nile River, we began to cry out for a land bathed in the blood of thousands of innocent people at the hands of satanically influenced rebels. By then the focus of our prayers had become to see this land washed with the powerful healing blood of Jesus as binding the brokenhearted and manifesting God's love and deliverance through signs and wonders.

What we found in this war-torn part of northern Uganda was worse than any of us could have imagined. I knew instantly, this was the place for me! There was not a single Western missionary there that I knew of; all had left a long time ago in the face of the satanic rampage of the rebels.

After we returned, I realized, in spite of the blessings during my time in Kampala so far, my heart still yearned to be sent where no one else wanted to go. I knew northern Uganda was the place. As time went on, I began to hear more and more horror stories of the terror inflicted by the Lord's Resistance Army (LRA) and their leader, Joseph Kony from some of those who had escaped the fighting and sought refuge at our mission. As they confirmed all western missionaries had long abandoned the area in the North, it confirmed to me that without a doubt, this was the place the Lord had for me on a permanent basis!

When my year at Lake Victoria Christian Center came to an end, the missionary returned and I went back to the United States. This time it was different. There was no question, I knew I would return and be sent to Northern Uganda. My heart was filled with joy and anticipation as I shared with others about my mission. Their reaction was one of horror and fear. I couldn't blame them because without the Lord I knew I wouldn't survive. At the same time, I was absolutely certain that with Him, I could not fail.

One night, as I was praying on my bed, I felt a hand pull me into a sitting position with a sudden force. I heard a voice saying, "Ten said 'no'. Two said 'go'. I will give you a promised land. Bloodshed, slaughter and giants will be your Canaan land, but the fruit will be big."

"Who is going to send me, Lord?"

There was no answer, but I knew He would make a way where there was no way. The next day, I contacted the American

Embassy to inquire if they allowed American citizens to go to northern Uganda.

"That is Joseph Kony's territory and a place where no one wants to go. Do not go."

"Is this a suggestion or an order?" I asked.

"It is a strong suggestion. If you insist on going, we will cross you off the list."

"What does that mean?"

"There is no chance for you to return to this country except in a body bag."

After I hung up the phone, I contacted several Christian organizations to see if they would consider sending me. They laughed and told me all their missionaries had long since pulled out because it was suicide to stay. In spite of this, I knew I had found the place I had been praying for. During my stay before, I had fallen in love with the Acholi people and began to see God's vision for bringing his glory out of ashes in that country.

Since no one else dared to support me, I decided to ask my pastor. He was a man of God and I trusted him to hear from the Lord. After we prayed together, he looked at me with a smile and said, "What would Paul have done? Go. We will lay hands on you and send you in the Name of the Lord." I had my confirmation.

Two widow ladies agreed to support me and a man from a prayer group gave me enough money to buy a car. During the short two months before I was to leave, an African Bishop came to speak at our church. He shared that he needed $400.00 to pay for his return ticket in 24 hours. As we prayed for him, the Lord spoke to me, "Give him your $400.00."

"This is all the money I have, Lord," I said under my breath as I handed it to the Bishop.

That evening, the man who gave me the money for the car approached me.

"Is there anything you need before you go, Carole?" he asked me.

"I am believing God for the ticket money."

"Come by the prayer center tomorrow."

When I met him the next day, he gave me enough for the ticket and a computer. My God supplies all my needs!

When the day of my departure finally arrived, it was hard to say goodbye to my three daughters. Although they were grown, I would miss them terribly. The enormity of my decision weighed on me when I hugged them at the airport. At that moment, my oldest daughter slipped a piece of paper in my hand as we hugged. It had a scripture from Acts 26:19 which says,

I was not disobedient to the vision from heaven.

The Lord was reassuring me to be obedient and not give in to fear. It renewed my resolve to go and I felt His anointing as I stepped on the plane, chosen by God to bring His love, light and deliverance to a people held in bondage and fear for so many years. To this day, I carry that piece of paper in my Bible.

As my thoughts returned to tonight's horrors, I opened my eyes and the light from the flames of the burning huts shone through the small window of my tiny bedroom dancing like tongues of fire on the wall. The screams had stopped and an eerie silence had taken its place. Strangely, there was no fear in my heart that the rebels might burn my tiny house; just a peaceful feeling I would be needed in the morning to give comfort and aid to the many that had lost their homes and maybe their loved ones.

"Give me the strength, the love and the mercy to be there for them, Lord," I prayed before I drifted off to sleep.

The air was filled with smoke when I stepped out of the house. It was early and the sun had not quite come up over the horizon. Most of the huts were smoldering heaps of black ashes in the misty, gray air of early dawn. The lone figure of a woman, her head buried between her knees, cowered in front of one of the huts a small distance away. It had been her home only yesterday. A small boy stood next to her, his face a blank stare as he looked at me without making a sound. His eyes were empty as he stared at nothing in particular in silence. The woman raised her head up slowly when she heard me approach.

"Mama, what am I going to do? The fire killed my little girl and the soldiers took the two older boys." Her voice sounded dead.

"Where is your husband?" I asked.

"The soldiers took him a few days ago on his way back from the market here in Gulu. I have not heard from him since." She reached out for the little boy and held him close to her. "He is all I have left," she added with resignation. "There is nothing else." She pointed behind her to the smoldering heap of her hut with a helpless gesture. "Nothing."

"Come with me to the ministry. Someone will take care of you there," I said as I held out my hand.

This is why I had come. I felt I belonged here for this time and to the people called the Acholis, abandoned by the world, but not by God. Gulu is situated in the North of Uganda. The name 'Gulu' means "Pot" in the Acholi language, because it sits in the depression of a floodplain. Uganda's capital city is Kampala. Gulu district is composed of Aswa County, Omoro County and Gulu Municipal Council. Ninety percent of the population in 2002 had sought refuge in what was referred to as 'Internally Displaced People Camps' which house between ten and sixty thousand people.

These were made up of men, women and children unable to work the land for the last twenty years because of the fighting between the government forces and Joseph Kony's Lord Resistance Army. The resulting poverty and starvation was unimaginable and thousands succumbed to its grip. Sometimes, I even wondered how God with His unlimited power could overcome the evil in this hellish place and all I could do was believe He would, since He sent me here.

At the time I started the ministry in the North in early 2004, the Uganda People's Defense Force had launched a massive military offensive against the LRA bases in neighboring southern Sudan. In retaliation, the LRA attacked the IDP camps and villages in northern Uganda, brutally killing, raping and destroying hundreds and thousands of defenseless people.

As if that was not enough, over 35,000 children, mostly between the ages of eight and fifteen were abducted by Kony's rebels, taken to camps and turned into cold-blooded killing machines through brutal and inhumane 'training' methods.

The Ugandan Ministry of Health estimated that during those years, of the more than two million people living in more than 200 camps in Northern Uganda, 1,000 died weekly from malaria, starvation, ambushes and AIDS. Not counting the thousands who were killed outside the camps across the countryside by the rebels.

This was the place God had sent me; a hellish, brutal area, filled with unspeakable terror, cruelty and suffering. Totally unimaginable to my western mind. In my human understanding, there was no way I would or could ever survive this inferno, being a sole white woman in the entire region. Yet, I had no doubt God had sent me with the mandate to reach out to a people the world had forgotten by telling them of His love for them and bring healing and wholeness to this nation. Only He could defeat an enemy who had reigned supreme for generations. His real name was not Joseph Kony, but Satan!

How could any country possibly get to this place? The reason was simple, the principalities and powers of the enemy had never been dislodged and neither had there ever been a full generation of Christian teaching and discipleship in this nation. Many times missionaries came, but were dispelled by war and bloodshed before they could make an inroad, because they did not know how to come against the stronghold of Satan and his demons.

Joseph Kony, the leader of the LRA, had declared himself Jesus Christ and a worshipper of Satan. The majority of the people in each town and village had been subjugated by Shamans and witch doctors, who rule them with an iron hand. The supernatural power of Satan was quite evident in everyday life, while the power of God had nearly been extinguished by the presence of evil.

There was no doubt in my mind, one lone white woman in this sea of evil and destruction could do nothing unless my all-powerful God and His Holy Spirit went ahead of me, protected me and let His miracle power change a world from pure evil to one of righteousness, peace and joy in the Name of Jesus Christ.

The day finally arrived when I left Lake Victoria Christian Center and set out on the six-hour drive north to Gulu. As I traveled with my African team members, the Spirit of God began to move upon our hearts, even in the car.

As we crossed the Nile River, we began crying out for a land drowning in the blood of thousands of innocent people at the hands of satanically influenced rebels. We longed to see this land washed with the powerful healing blood of Jesus. Binding the brokenhearted and manifesting God's love and deliverance through signs and wonders would be the focus of our prayers in the camps.

Five pastors and a group of Christians welcomed me into the tiny house. It had cement floors with a small living area with wooden chairs and a table. The bedroom was furnished with a single, wooden bed covered by a foam mattress. Praise the Lord, there was a bathroom! Since the power lines were down, there was no electricity. The kitchen consisted of a charcoal cooking area outside. All clothes had to be washed by hand. My little house was the only one made of brick in the area, while all the others were mud huts along a dirt road.

Later on, they introduced me to the believers in the town. For the first time I realized *I really was the only westerner in this entire area!* This reality shocked me. *When I asked You to send me where no one wants to go, You took me up on it, didn't You, Lord?* I thought.

"This will do fine," I said with as much bravado as I could muster.

"I know you are used to better," one of the pastors said. He stood and looked down at his feet, hesitating, "Are you going to take pictures and stay here a little while and tell of the bullets

18

flying and then go back to your country and make money on making movies from our suffering like some others have done?"

I looked at him, astonished and ashamed of how they had been exploited by other westerners in years past and managed to say, "I didn't come here to sow a seed, I came to sow my life."

In a very short time I realized they would never be able to be true leaders unless they learned to trust not only me, but their Father in Heaven as sons. I started to hold retreats once a month and invited not only them, but their wives as well. I taught them to tithe, helped repair their roofs and taught them to take care of orphans.

I put a cardboard sign on the little gate in our front yard saying, 'House of Prayer' 7:00 am and 7:00 pm, 7 days a week-all are welcome.

Soon word got around and the little house in Gulu became a House of Prayer and prayer retreats for pastors and team leaders. In time, inspired by what they learned, they risked going back and forth to very dangerous camps with the gospel. Gulu Town, where I lived, was in the middle of the war area. From there, the team leaders I was training, traveled to over a hundred different camps of displaced Acholi refugees all across the North. Each camp had a population of ten to seventy-five thousand people, all desperately in need of Jesus. My heart was enlarged, as well as broken into a million pieces. But this was now my home. Would I survive? My trust was in my Father who brought me here.

One of the Displaced People's Camps

Typical Village Life in Uganda

Chapter 2

Dancing with Lepers

I don't know whether it was a dream or a vision. I was praying for the many unreached people in Uganda in what seemed to be the crying room of a church. I was busy helping to dress a beautiful bride. She stood radiant and perfect, wearing a magnificent gown of expensive material. When I stepped back to look at her, to my horror, I discovered her feet were covered in mud and filth.

"What am I going to do?" I cried out in a loud voice.

"Wash them the way Mary Magdalene washed My feet."

As I bent my head, tears started streaming down my face and splashed onto her feet. With my hair, I wiped them dry until her feet were perfectly clean.

"Only the heart of a Eunuch can wash My feet."

"Why a Eunuch, Lord?"

"There are so many hirelings who are soiling and raping the bride."

Looking through a window into a church sanctuary, Father God was standing at the front. The church was packed with people. I saw Jesus coming in, His face filled with joyful anticipation for His bride. He turned to the Father and said, "I can't wait to see her."

After I finished wiping her feet, I slid her beautiful slippers on and then watched as she walked down the aisle of the church toward Jesus. Before she reached Him, many doors opened and other brides from different countries and nationalities joined her, dressed in exactly the same dress, just different colors of skin. The Lord stretched out His arms and welcomed them with a radiant smile. Before they reached Him, the many brides merged

21

into one. When His united, beloved bride drew close, she was bathed in the soft glow of His love as Jesus took her hand and together they turned and stood before the Father.

I instantly knew God was branding my heart in the shape of this nation, knowing without a doubt, northern Uganda was the bride I was supposed to help dress for Him because on her own she did not know she was His bride.

"I will call them my people who are not my people; and I will call her 'my loved one who is not my loved one,…"
Romans 9:25

Only through God's eyes was I able to find the beautiful garment of His love in this dark place, with a people bent on destroying each other with an unimaginable hatred and bloodshed, spawned in the pit of hell itself. My heart broke as I walked in and out of some of the 150 IDS camps, trying desperately to relieve the suffering of at least some of the thousands who lived there.

Over one thousand died daily from starvation, disease and ambushes. The total lack of facilities was painfully evident as I sidestepped feces covering the ground everywhere. The stench was overwhelming and hung thick over the countless, flimsy tents in the humid, hot air. Some camps were made up of hundreds of tiny shelters a few feet off the ground that were built with rice sacks draped over 4 sticks. Family members crawled under these gunny sack shelters in hopes strong rains wouldn't pelt them to the ground, leaving them running for a small, crowded covering under mango trees or other overhangs.

Some of these camps received humanitarian aid through food distribution once every two months. The amount delivered to each family was barely enough to feed them for a week. Many attempted to go back and garden in their villages, trying to bring home enough food for their children, never to return back alive. The rebel attacks in the villages were the most numerous, but they also happened in these camps guarded by the military as well. A borehole, or water well, was the only source of water for thousands of people, and cholera runs rampant along with AIDS in these crowded and unsanitary conditions.

I could not believe this had been the home for hundreds of thousands of refugees for the last eighteen years, their lives void of hope and security. They had been driven from their villages by the rebels, leaving behind any chance of a normal life as they buried the corpses of their loved ones. Many of their children had been abducted by the soldiers without the chance of ever returning while the world looked on and did nothing.

"I want to live in the camps and live with the people there, Lord. How can I help them if I can't feel what they feel?" I had cried so many times. "How do they sleep with the constant horror? How can I stop the bullets, the witchcraft and the brutal godlessness in this land?"

Psalm 91 came to my mind and I knew God had answered. They must learn the secret place of the Most High God and how deep His love is for each of them.

Not long after, we started working in Keyo camp by reaching out to the people with food, clothes and the Gospel. While it was a small beginning, I knew the Lord would be with me, keep me safe and guide me as I went. His love would have to be the light in the darkness and His compassion a ray of hope in this horrible hopelessness.

One day, I came across a section reserved for people with leprosy. I will never forget the man who reached out his stubbed hands to me with a smile as I walked by. His toes and fingers were gone and he was unable to feed himself or walk properly. Yet there was something about his face, filled with hope and trust as he stretched out his deformed arms to me. It was as if he could see Jesus and His love for him through me. It touched me deeply.

He was not the only one. As I walked on, I found many more like him, sitting in abject misery, hunger and hopelessness along the dirt road filled with sewage and garbage. My mind reeled with a mixture of repulsion, sorrow, empathy and love as I tried hard to ignore the stench and avoid the worst of the feces in the road.

It was impossible for me to shake the gruesome sights after I got home that evening and I began to travail for this country and its people. As tears soaked my pillow, I came against the satanic power of the 120 witches and warlocks in this area alone, who were stoking the fires of violence, hatred and murder throughout the land. My heart broke as I thought of the many children who were dedicated to 'the spirits' from birth in this land where Satan reigned supreme and operated in darkness through this leader called Joseph Kony.

Without the power of God, there was no way I could ever survive here, least of all win the souls of those who wanted to give their lives to Christ. I wondered how the Lord was going to use me to accomplish the impossible.

During the night, I had a vision. I was dancing with Jesus in a beautiful waltz. He was swinging me around, and we were lost in the rhythm of the worship. All of a sudden, it wasn't Jesus dancing with me, it was the leper I met in the camp. His smile was radiant as he led me in a twirling waltz, singing and worshiping at the same time. There was no repulsion in me as we danced; just a deep joy to be with him.

"Watch," Jesus said.

It was then I saw the other seventy join us in the dancing with singing and rejoicing.

"If you dance with the lepers, I will heal them."

From then on, I visited many of the camps, following the food trucks since they were heavily guarded by government soldiers. Others from the ministry were too afraid to drive with me when the convoys were not running. I decided to drive alone in spite of the danger of frequent, violent roadside ambushes by the rebels. We were only allowed to drive between ten in the morning and four in the afternoon, because the rebel attacks were heightened before and after those times. That gave us only six hours a day to minister to the people in the camps.

It was on one of those early trips that I drove alone in my car on the long way to the camp through isolated bush country, without a single patrol. Filled with fear, I constantly looked left and right, trying to spot men with AK 47's waiting for me along the side of the road, knowing the rebels would torture and kill me without hesitation.

"I never send anyone out in fear." The voice of the Lord was clear. "You are living in self-preservation instead of self-denial."

"You would be afraid, too, Lord," I answered. "These rebels need no excuse to kill me."

"You need more love, because, "Perfect love casts out fear," was His answer. (1 John 4:18) "If you lay your life down, I will baptize you in love, for it says in My Word, "Greater love has no one than this: to lay down one's life for one's friends." John 15:13.

"Baptize me in Your love, Lord."

Suddenly, waves of liquid peace and emotion surged through me. I had trouble driving as I felt a strong urge to wrap my arms around this nation, pulling to myself the broken, hurt and devastated people and presenting them to the heart of God. In an instant I understood, they did not need a sermon, they needed to know there is a God and He has arms. He had sent me to show them by using mine.

I started to cry, not with tears of sorrow, but of joy. I was no longer afraid and knew I would never be again, because the perfect love He had given me for the Acholi people *had* cast out all fear from that day on.

As I walked among the refugees in the camps, one thing struck me – the deadness in their eyes, the lack of emotion in their faces and the abject hopelessness in the way they moved. It was as if the dead had come to life, but with their soul missing. The light in their hearts had gone out because of the prolonged cruelty of their tortured existence. Satan had successfully killed them while still living.

I knew I could never fully understand their pain, but I was sure God did and I felt He had chosen me to help set His people free; not with guns and tanks, but by His love. Personally, I would not have chosen a single woman from a far-away country, without money, power or connections if I had anything to say about it. But then, how better to show His power and love than through a weak vessel like me to defeat Satan and his forces in a country devastated by evil?

This was brought home to me when a young man named Opio walked into the mission house, homeless, broken and starving. His story tells of how God rescued him from the horrors of Joseph Koney's rebel camp to become a warrior in God's Army instead. His life shows the limitless power of prayer along with transformation through the Word of God which turned Opio's life around. I will let him tell his story in his own words.

Opio

"My father was captured by Kony's LRA rebels before my birth in 1984. Because my mother could not raise me, I was taken to my grandmother's village to be cared for by her. By the time my 12th birthday came, my mother had died of AIDS. At

26

the age of 15, as I was sleeping in my grandmother's village hut with a friend, the LRA rebels attacked at 3:00 am. My friend and I were abducted, taken into the bush and beaten 150 times with sticks. We were threatened that if we ever escaped, we would be killed. I lay unconscious for over a day from the beatings, but when I recovered, I was given a chopped human head to carry for 35 miles on foot. This was to make us brave and prepare us for the inhumane acts the rebels would teach us to do. We were taken to Sudan for 2 months training, which included making us drink animal blood mixed with human blood while the sign of the cross was printed across our bodies. After that we were wrapped with human intestines and made to jump over rotting human bodies. We were tormented with fear and threats of being killed if we ever thought of escaping. From 1999 to 2003, I moved with Kony's rebels throughout northern Uganda, where I was involved in ambushes, village raids and massacres. I burned huts, and learned to abduct and even kill my own tribal people. During one raid, as we were attacking a village, I received a bullet wound to my foot. My chest and eye were also wounded.

As I ran with a bleeding foot, trying to escape the fighting, I met a commander from the Ugandan military who told me I had been wounded because of the bad things I was doing, and that if I didn't stop and surrender, I would die. I was already thinking about my grandmother back home, but had been warned by the rebels that all my living relatives had been killed and I would be as well if I tried to escape. I ran 23 miles with the bloody wound in my foot and the bullet still lodged in it.

A kind doctor was finally able to remove it almost a month after my injury. In 2003, I was sent with 17 other young men armed with guns to ambush vehicles on the road to the camp of Kitgum and other villages. During one of the raids, we abducted 10 Acholi villagers from the camp of Pabo. As we were in the bush that evening with our prisoners, I was ordered to take 2 of them to fetch water. Walking with them to the watering hole, I questioned one of the men, "Do rebels who surrender ever go back home or are they shot or made to drink poison?" The man stepped close and answered, almost weeping, "If you only knew that you could get help in Gulu town if you surrendered, you wouldn't be suffering like this. Many surrendering rebels come out of the bush and are being cared for." This man's kindness touched my heart and I set the 2 prisoners free, telling them to look for me in town soon.

Back at the rebel camp in the bush, none of the soldiers asked me what happened to my prisoners. They just assumed I had killed them. The next morning as our detachment was marching deep in the bush past a swamp, I told the other soldiers to go on ahead. I quietly dropped my gun next to the swamp, took some sugar and combat boots, and started running as fast as I could towards smoke I saw rising from a far-away village.

When I came to a river, I bathed, threw away my rebel uniform and combed my long, unkempt hair with a metal instrument. Then I threw away the rosary and olive oil Kony's commander had given me, and I cried out loud, "You demonic spirits of Kony depart from me. I am now a different person!" I ran until I saw a man and his wife farming near a village. When they saw me, they dropped their tools in fear and started running. I yelled, "Stop, brother, please help me." The man came back and wanted to know if I was from the bush and if I was alone. I assured him I was and pleaded with him for help. He took me to a UPDF – Ugandan military detachment where they kept me for 2 days to debrief me. I didn't eat during those days, because I thought they would poison me. I just took the sugar I had brought with me from the bush and mixed it with water.

I was taken by the military to the World Vision Children of War Rehabilitation Center in Gulu for 3 months of trauma counseling. It was there I gave my life to Jesus Christ and accepted Him as my personal Savior. In June 2003, I was finally released back to my own village. Finding out my grandmother had died, I moved in with an uncle and aunt. I started going to a little church in Gulu town, where I was allowed to help with the children. I love working with children because I know the Kingdom of heaven is for people who are just like them. I prayed that God would save my family and give me a new direction for my life. I asked God to forgive me for the terrible things I had done in the north as a rebel and to change me so I would never be the same again.

In February 2004, I went to a Portable Bible school in Gulu for 2 months and my life has never been the same since then. I praise God for that school because it brought revival to my heart and showed me God's forgiveness. I began to learn the Word of God and understand His purpose for my life.

My prayer now is that Jesus will use me to serve Him in any way I can as it is my greatest desire God will change our nation in Jesus' name. All I came through was by the grace of Jesus. I would have died if He had not been by my side. I praise Him because I will never be the same again since Hc found me and rescued me."

A smile transformed Opio's face as he ended his story by telling of the saving deliverance of a mighty, merciful God! He radiated the love and compassion of Jesus and became one of the leaders of our Acholi children's choir in Gulu and sang with great conviction of the love of God as he played one of the native harps made from animal skins and hair. Opio went through one of our workshops to learn children's ministry and worked with the child evangelism team in the town's bus park. Later, he joined our staff at the House of Prayer in Gulu for the prayer retreats we had there. This is where he helped to lead worship as he skillfully played his African harp and where we got to share wonderful times of prayer with him, asking for God's perfect direction for his life. He became my first son and a strong leader in the ministry with his powerful testimony of what God did, not just for him, but for so many others as well as they listened to him.

Eventually, I was able to enroll him in the small vocational school where he learned masonry skills, something which had been a great desire of his heart along with serving in children's ministry. We became Opio's family and he learned to pray earnestly for other young rebels in the same situation he had been in, to see them surrender and find new identity in Jesus Christ.

Opio's story shows that in God's Kingdom 'love truly covers a multitude of sins,' (1Peter 4:8) and no one, not even the most broken, is beyond the Lord's redemptive mercy. It is a wonderful example of how God accomplished the impossible, changing pure evil in the hearts and minds of so many young men into the righteousness of Christ through God's unconditional love and forgiveness. In amazement, I watched change come to this seemingly forsaken nation, not through armies and guns, but through saving, restoring and renewing one heart at a time.

What a privilege it has been to be a part of this astounding miracle of the resurrection of a nation over the past few years. What a wonderful chance to have been a part of God's power in action as the Holy Spirit swept over the land, defeating the enemy on a grand scale such as has never been seen before.

But I am getting ahead of myself.

Fervent, Persistent Prayer

Chapter 3

Fire Meets Sacrifice
With our Faces in the Dirt

I soon came to realize the Lord had not sent me to this land to do battle with conventional, human weapons. Nor was my main purpose to clothe and feed the poor, but He sent me to take part in a spiritual battle with an enemy who was far stronger than Joseph Kony and his rebel army. Like in Daniel, chapters 9 and 10, God expected me to take part in a spiritual warfare to break down the stronghold of the ruling spirit holding the land in captivity. This battle would be fought in the spiritual realm, by heaven's forces, as Daniel saw, and by the supernatural power of God rather than bullets and tanks.

On my part, it would take more than just regular prayers, more than just standing in the gap or crying out alone. It would take a people, desperate, but not in despair. Weak, but not without power, and ready to wrestle in the mighty Name of Jesus, resisting forces of darkness that had ruled this territory for a long time. Instead of speaking to the mountain, it would require us to blow the mountain to pieces, learning what it meant for 'the Kingdom suffers violence, but the violent take it by force.' We needed the kind of desperation which produced spiritual dynamite for God's kingdom, and the land.

The little mission house started to fill up with people who came to pray from 7AM till 7PM every day, crying out for God to show His hand. In spite of it, there was a sense in all of us; it was not enough to push back the enemy in the land.

"What do you want me to do, Lord?" I asked as a subtle feeling of despair tried to get hold of me. "We have done all we know how to do. Why doesn't the deep darkness have to go?"

The picture of the little stadium in Gulu came into my mind. It had been used as a War Memorial Stadium, which was literally a graveyard for British and Acholi soldiers during colonial wars. No bigger than a football field, it was surrounded by a stone wall. This would be the first time the grounds had ever been allowed to be used by the government for prayer. Three times in the past, the people of the town had defied the authorities and had gathered there, yet each time tragedy had struck in the form of accidental deaths and other mishaps. I realized the enemy would come against us if I did the same by defying the authorities. Yet when I asked permission, they turned me down. Instead of giving up, I called the prayer warriors together, and after days of fasting and coming against the evil forces in the Name of Jesus, I approached government leaders again for the use of the grounds. This time they miraculously agreed without hesitation. Praise God!

I knew a revival of prayer was needed! Not only of prayer, but united and repentant prayer, coupled with the authority of God's Word and the turning of our hearts back to godly principles. This is what we began praying and fasting for across Gulu. Forty days of prayer chains were mobilized within the local churches and the House of Prayer on the ground, preceding the prayer gathering in the Acholi War Memorial Stadium. I wanted to reach out beyond Gulu and the local area and contacted radio stations around the nation, inviting believers from all over Uganda to stand together in a united heart cry for the peace of the nation as well as the upcoming elections, which were extremely critical for national revival. The word of our three-day prayer gathering spread like wildfire across the land and nationally known prayer leaders contacted us to join our effort, offering to lead different sessions of prayer. Political figures agreed to represent their area by lifting their hands in heartfelt intercession during this time.

The Lord showed me we should come together as one Body of Christ for this part of His Body called Northern Uganda, to be healed, restored and reach its full potential in God's eternal purpose.

Prayer chains around the clock were set up across the area, coupled with fasting. The intensity and devotion in the hearts of those who took part was overwhelming. With great expectations for seeing the hand of God to move in a mighty way, we finally watched the day approach as the Gulu National Prayer Gathering finally arrived on December 15, 2005.

It was an incredible time of intense, united and desperate intercession, crying out for God to work His deliverance in this land. Pastors and church leaders who hadn't spoken to each other in years because of the divisions in the body of Christ here in the north, came together to work in one accord. Over 1,000 people gathered for three days of prayer and for the first time in the humble, little stadium in Gulu, cries went up for revival in the land, the upcoming national elections and for the presence of God as the Prince of Peace to return to Northern Uganda. In an atmosphere of worship, passages of scripture were read during each session, followed by over an hour of prayer for each request.

It's almost as if we could hear the angels of heaven worshipping with us as the field was scattered with heaven-hungry saints on their faces in the grass, pacing the land and crying out to God as they gathered in clusters and countless groups, agreeing in powerful prayer. We could sense the intensity; the heartfelt repentance and the faith that rose from the grounds during those days. It was as if God opened the windows of heaven and poured out His love and healing power over this wounded broken land in an unprecedented way.

Throughout those three days, I saw His hand move in a mighty way beyond what I could ever have imagined. It was too wonderful for me to comprehend how He could use weak, humble vessels to push back the enemy and open the doors for restoration, healing and spiritual freedom as never before.

34

Pastors stated that they sensed heaven opening in a new way. Government leaders called and testified of a strong sense that the spiritual climate over the area had changed. Miracles were reported from the local churches the following week in the form of countless salvations and miraculous provision. Glory be to God for He IS a rewarder of those who diligently seek Him! All of us felt this was only the beginning of what would follow.

The stadium prayer gathering proved to be a 'gateway' for further prayer gatherings in Gulu. Citywide intercession sprang up in a new and powerful way as people were coming out of isolation and beginning to pray together.

The following January was set aside as a month of prayer in the town to cover the coming year with divine direction and a continual yearning for transforming revival. Seven houses of prayer were established in seven camps in January and February by the prayer teams with the vision of continuing to plant such prayer houses in every camp in the north as quickly as possible. These prayer houses were coupled with teaching on united and informed prayer that would continue seven days a week and be led collectively by the pastors we were working with in each camp.

The Sunday after the prayer gathering, we were back in the camp of Opit. As four little churches met together under the trees, singing and praising, the power of the Word was preached in the open air. It was received with hunger and joy. As believers testified of deep and aching burdens for their children and grandchildren still in captivity, of suffering with mental illness and torment because of the atrocities of this war, we wept with them, embracing them in their pain. We offered the only, but greatest hope we had, the healing love and comfort of His precious Holy Spirit. As I waved good-bye to these heroes of faith, I lifted my heart again to the Father, and within me cried out, "You must move, dear God!! You must heal!! You must restore!! Hear the heart cries of your people, even as you did the Israelites in bondage, and rend the heavens for your own Name's sake!!! He alone IS faithful!"

Because this war was such a spiritual one, we knew the answer lay with God and God alone. We knew we had to act and not keep silent but go forward with the gospel while there was time. I realized, as camps began to scatter over the next few years and people returned to their villages, we would miss the opportunity to reach so many multitudes who are gathered in such small spaces. If I ever felt an urgency of the Holy Spirit to 'work for the night is coming, when no man shall work anymore...' it was then. I knew if we were ever to see the 'Gospel Go'- in the form of portable Bible schools, houses of prayer, clothing and Bible distribution, youth and children's camps, health training and reading classes, teaching and discipleship training, crusades and door to door evangelism, this was the time to lay the groundwork. The scripture in Isaiah 60:1-3 filled my heart when I thought back to the stadium prayer and what the Lord was doing,

"Arise and shine; for their light has come! And the glory of the Lord has risen upon them. For behold the darkness shall cover the earth, and deep darkness the people; but the Lord will arise over them. And His glory will be seen upon them. And Gentiles will come to their light and kings to the brightness of their rising."

By the end of that year, we sent a team of 12 to the camp of Ocet teaching and evangelizing. This camp was in the district where Kony grew up, and had been neglected spiritually, as well as socially, by agencies in many ways, due to the fear that presides over the area. It was a large camp with intense spiritual darkness and only a few struggling little churches. They organized prayer and intercession teams among the believers on the ground and started door-to-door evangelism, together with Bible classes and Bible study methods coupled with Bible distribution. As we distributed clothing following outdoor evening evangelistic crusades, many people gave their lives to Jesus. While this time was productive, the spiritual atmosphere proved hard to penetrate.

36

Around the camp, shrines still stood, where sacrifices were made to goat and other animal gods. Occult practices were rampant in this area where four districts connect their corners-Apac, Gulu, Pader, and Lira. But praise His Name, in spite of this, the church was strengthened, believers were added to the body of Christ, discipleship went forth powerfully, and the ground was prepared in a new way for the upcoming Portable Bible School sessions we were planning for the coming year.

In time, we came to realize, the stadium prayer, as it had come to be known, was the pivotal turning point for Northern Uganda. Even government officials openly admitted that this prayer gathering paved the way to the end of the war by pushing back the powers of darkness, and beginning to restore the land one soul at a time. It started the process of rebuilding His Body through prayer being established in EVERY life, EVERY hut, EVERY camp and EVERY little church in all of Northern Uganda so His glory might come and His will be done on earth as it is in heaven! Houses of prayer were being set up and strengthened in strategically located IDP camps all over the north. Believers were coming together in a new way, not just struggling for survival anymore, but with a fresh revelation of the Father's love, of who they were in Christ, and of their position with Him in heavenly places, and so tear down the gates of hell and see the prisoners set free! Teaching was going forth along with united prayer, and the vision was to see 24-hour prayer chains in all 150 camps covering northern Uganda in order that hell would be plundered and God's Kingdom established in every community!

Once a month, we were bringing pastors in from the camps for teaching, breaking bread together, and the refreshment and empowering of an overnight prayer and praise gathering that sent them back on their one to three hour bike ride to their camps-refreshed and envisioned to gather believers with a new zeal to pray and to do the works of the Master.

In the camp of Opit with 50,000 plus people and the second largest camp in the north, we graduated 110 students from a two-month intensive Bible school. There was door to door evangelism which allowed many to hear the gospel and coming into the Kingdom of God. We established a children's camp with Bible studies, sports, and singing; a medical outreach with free dental care which had never been available in the camps since the beginning of the war. The Jesus film was shown in Acholi, reaching multitudes with the gospel message of salvation. There was Bible distribution with Bible study training classes; clothing distribution; intercessory prayer training and intensive Bible study. God's Word along with the power of prayer was the Truth setting the captives free! The atmosphere was electrifying as graduates shouted with joy at the receiving of their Training Certificates and a new Bible. The power of God's love transformed lives and was beginning to shake hell's gates wide open in northern Uganda, a country where no one wanted to go!

The future of Uganda

Love conquers all

"Let the children come to me…"

Chapter 4

Treasures of Darkness

I was driving on the bumpy dirt road back to Gulu from one of the camps, when I met hundreds of children walking on foot, on their way to Gulu town. Like they did every night, they had spent the night there to escape possible rebel attacks. What would they find when they got back home in the morning; burning huts, their mother and father abducted or worse, dead?

I saw some of them digging in a termite mound for small insects, eating them live from the nests. Others sat by the side of the road and held out their hands toward me, begging while resting from the long walk. As I drove on, another group was digging up cassava roots or eating raw vegetable leaves to still their gnawing hunger. While they could find safety in the guarded areas in Gulu for the night, there was no food there, just temporary shelter to escape from being abducted or killed.

I knew, many children, orphaned by the tragedy of AIDS, lived without parental protection in their village and struggled alone to survive. These were called the 'child headed huts'. Sometimes there were 5-12 children crowded together in one tiny dilapidated mud hut, trying to find food, or sell stick brooms for a few coins to buy a scrap of food.

I could only imagine the constant fear they lived with because many of their friends or neighbors had disappeared, never to be seen again. Kony's LRA rebels were after the children. They made 'better soldiers' we were told, than the adults. They ate less, were easier to brain wash, obeyed faster, and killed easier, not knowing the finality of death. When they were abducted, the boys were sent north into Sudan to be trained for terrorist warfare, and the girls were used as concubines for the soldiers or sold into slavery in Sudan, experiencing cruel brutalities. That is why these children traveled by foot from scattered villages each evening to the town of Gulu, where they slept protected by the Ugandan army from rebel attacks.

At dusk each evening, they walked barefoot, five to eight kilometers into town where they slept on the ground or on a thin blanket or straw mat. Some were under temporary shelters or large government tents, and many just under the stars at night, praying it wouldn't thunderstorm that evening. In the morning, they would walk the distances back to their villages trying to find enough food to eat to make it through the day before they repeated the journey again that evening.

I felt utter astonishment and horror, watching for the first time, as fifteen thousand children walked to the town of Gulu from surrounding villages each evening to sleep on the ground where they found military protection from the rebels' attacks. Some children were given a blanket to spread on the ground at night but none of them were fed. The desire to help them, feed and clothe them was overwhelming in me but the sheer number made it seem like a hopeless undertaking.

There were 150 different camps for displaced war victims. Each had desolate conditions with one water hole for 5,000 people, where cholera, TB, AIDS, HIV and starvation was rampant. Once again, there was no doubt in my mind, only God could help me know where to start with this magnitude of suffering children, many of whom were orphaned due to AIDS or massacres.

My heart burned within me as I drove by and a feeling of helplessness overwhelmed me as I watched them. I felt powerless to change their lives. Or was I?

"Lord, have mercy on these children," I prayed. "They belong to You. In Your love, look on them as Your treasures of darkness, precious in Your sight and every one worth saving. You sent me here, help me to turn their darkness into light and their suffering into joy." I was crying as my car continued to pass by the many small figures, walking slowly down the dusty road, their eyes filled with an empty hopelessness. They never looked up at me, but moved in silence, too tired and hungry to notice me.

That night I laid awake as the trek of children passed in my mind's eye.

"What is it You want me to do, Lord? Tell me and I will do it."

'Open a children's home for them. Feed them, and love them, even one. When you love them, you love Me. It is the only way you will see this nation change, one child at a time.'

The answer was so simple and yet the task seemed overwhelming when I thought of the sheer numbers, fifteen thousand of them, walking to this town from the surrounding villages each day! What difference could my small efforts possibly make? I had no funds to pay for this, no idea how to bring it about.

After seeking God earnestly and approaching some of the local pastors about the greatest need, I was told that the 'total orphans' were the ones with mom and dad both dead. That's where I would start.

Countless people joined us in prayer for heaven to be opened and move the hand of God to supply our needs.

"I don't have any support, money or place to house the children, Lord. How can I possibly do what You are asking me to do?" I cried out with them.

"What do you have in your hands?"

"Nothing, Lord. All I have is a roof over my head," I answered.

That day I began to make room in my little house, including my bedroom. In faith, I took in four little girls, sisters, ages two, six, ten and twelve. There were many days we had only potatoes and water to eat and I slept on the floor. At that time, I still only lived on what the two widows sent each month. In prayer, the Lord impressed me one day, "Take the widows mite and turn it into the little boy's lunch and begin to share like he did at the feeding of the five thousand. I will multiply every resource. As you do, I will give you my heart beat and my compassion for the people. Learn to serve their vision and so unwrap their grave clothes. The healing of this land is within the heart of the people. Teach the Mamas and the widows to love the orphans, as I do. By doing this, I will use you to reach my people in this land."

One day, I was standing, looking out the back window of my little house. It was right after our first four little girls had moved in. I had been praying about who could be the first mama for our ministry. My eyes fell on Achang, a young girl in her early twenties. My mind went back six months ago to the first day she came into our mission house, during our early prayer time at seven in the morning.

Achang had walked by the house and stopped, drawn by the music. Filled with fear, yet compelled to enter, she walked around to the back door, entering reluctantly. As soon as she stepped over the threshold of the living room, she sank to her knees.

"I want what's in this house," she whispered.

I got up and hugged her.

"What is in this house is the love of the Lord Jesus. He has been waiting for you. Would you like to welcome Him into your heart?"

"I would."

After I prayed with her to receive Jesus, she looked at me with pleading eyes, "Can I stay here with you?"

"Where do you come from?" I asked.

She shrugged her shoulders in a helpless gesture and then told her story in a small voice, filled with pain.

"I was abducted at fourteen from my village, together with my brother who was twelve. We were taken to Sudan and trained by the LRA rebels in malicious, vicious, guerilla warfare and then sent back to Northern Uganda to fight with the rebel army. With our training with AK47's, we were forced to kill or be killed in

43

continuous battles. During this time, I was raped, mutilated and used as a sex slave by the rebels on a daily basis."

Her voice was a barely a whisper. I took her hand and said in a gentle tone, "It's alright, Achang, you are safe here."

"And then my brother was blown up during an eight-hour battle," she went on. "That evening, I overheard the soldiers talking. They had decided to kill me because my body was wasted and I had become useless to them. It was then I realized I could not stay because I was broken emotionally, physically and spiritually. I cried out to God,

"If You are real, help me escape."

I snuck out of the camp and then took off into the bush and ran for days. I only stopped to ask people in what direction Gulu was. In spite of my swollen and bleeding body, I kept on going until I stopped at your house."

She raised her head and with pleading eyes looked at me, "Please, don't send me away, I have nowhere to go."

During the next six months, she had time to heal from the horrible damage done to her insides, and her soul was touched by Jesus with His compassion and mercy.

My heart was filled with love and joy as I called her into the house that morning and asked her,

"Achang, would you like to be our first Mama?"

"Me?" she sounded incredulous.

"Yes," I answered with a smile.

"You really think I can do that?"

I put my arms around her and said with conviction, "I will believe in you until you can believe in yourself."

Achang is a part of the ministry to this day and is still the best Mama we ever had.

Soon, the word got around, "There really is a long-term home for these children in Gulu." People started coming, bringing children from 'child headed huts', or found on the body of a dead mother. One little boy was found beside the grave of his mother, weeping, and refusing to leave.

As the numbers grew, the Lord gave us clear directions and made a facility available in Gulu. In a giant step of faith, we began with a separate house and soon there were thirty-three total orphans in our care. Hundreds of others, who stayed with relatives who could not care for them, we helped outside the home by feeding and counseling them, as well as school and medical aid.

Because of the fear of terrorism during the last eighteen years, no one had ventured into this kind of work. Our vision of seeing God begin to mend their broken hearts was being fulfilled as He used them powerfully in being little prayer warriors and as members of healing teams to reach hundreds of children and adults in hospitals and in the camps.

God was true to His word and had provided all our needs!

The vision the Lord gave us was not just to reach out for the children but, with God's help, mend their broken hearts and minds in order to send them out some day in His power to reach thousands of others in the camps with the Gospel through signs and wonders. The precious 'victims of war' could become 'instruments of revival'.

As I shared the vision with friends in America and the funds started coming in, we knew a broken generation would be restored as part of God's plan to see His precious treasures redeemed and prepared to fulfill their destiny in His Kingdom.

A few years later, we were able to put a deposit down on 14 acres of land, to begin building a children's village in Gulu. When we sent out the written government proposal for licensing, the local authorities actually begged us to expand and enlarge the vision for these precious orphans to become future leaders in the nation.

The funds needed seemed overwhelming at the time, but our God was faithful. In time, we received the money needed to proceed and the House of Hope was established. Fully caring for broken, orphaned children, by feeding them, giving them medical care, education, counseling, spiritual training and emotional healing, and then raising them to be leaders, seemed like a huge job. It was amazing to watch as God transformed the many children He placed in our care. No matter the number or age, we were eager to be a part of His restoration in these many orphans' lives.

"Let the little children come to Me and do not forbid them; for to such is the kingdom of heaven." Matthew 19:14

The children grew into powerful prayer warriors and worshippers. Each evening, as they finished playing football in the compound, at 6:00, one of them would bang the African drum and they all came running. It was time for worship and this was the favorite part of their day.

Some children took to the African xylophone, others to the drums, and others to little hand-made 'shakers'. One child began to lead the singing and the others would follow. They danced enthusiastically in their tribal worship, until one child would break out in a passionate worship song. As they moved around the room, lost in love to their Father, they began to lift their little hands, weeping with love and gratitude, and putting one hand over their hearts in passionate worship. They began falling to their knees as the worship continued, until one would begin praying. Soon, they went from worship to prayer, in concert, and now on their faces, cried out to their heavenly Father for those children who were still in the 'bush' as rebel soldiers.

"Please free them, Lord. Please pull them out and bring them home." And because of these powerful and faith-filled prayers every single day, we watched God do that very thing as children escaped and came back to their villages, in search of their families.

The miracles these children witnessed through prayer, gave them faith to believe for greater and greater answers.

The story of precious little Akella, the youngest in our home, touched our hearts deeply. She was 3 years old, but looked to be the size of a one-year old. Her mother had died when she was born, leaving her to be raised by her ten-year-old sister. Because of lack of food or good nutrition, her growth was also stunted. She didn't speak, cried all the time and had numerous infections when she came. But within a few weeks of being in our home, her little heart began to heal and her spirit was quieted by the love poured out on her. God healed her infections and soon she started to talk, laugh and play. She was a joy to the staff and office team. Akella represents only two of the thousands of miracles God performed in countless other children just like them.

One day, we discovered Akella had a bone deficiency disease, because we noticed she slowly lost her ability to walk properly. Though we had her on calcium supplements and a good diet, her bones were mush from poor nutrition before and after birth. I took her to the best orthopedic surgeon I could find in Kampala. He confirmed our greatest fear, "I'm sorry, we can't fix her legs. We can screw plates on the sides of both her knees, but we would be screwing them into bone mush. There's no density."

I begged him to try anyway, and told him the children and I would pray. His heart was moved and he did as I asked. The children and I prayed every day but, in spite of two more surgeries, Akella was having trouble walking again. This time, the doctor told me, she would never walk.

"But we're going to pray for her, Mama", her thirty-two brothers and sisters said. "If Jesus heals others, He can heal our sister, too."

Their faith astounded me, and I agreed. To my amazement, they wanted to pray and fast as they had watched us do in the mission house. Every Wednesday, they requested they might be allowed to fast for their sister, Akella, and I sent notes to their teachers at school, telling them this was their request, not anyone forcing them. The children prayed violently and earnestly, and after one year of praying daily, and fasting every Wednesday, Akella's legs straightened up and she began walking normally, until one day, she simply joined the others in playing football.

That miracle, gave us all faith to believe the Father for anything in prayer.

Jesus had shown us by healing Akella's body what He was doing for the people across this land, as He touched their lives and raised their spirit and their bodies from the ashes of evil. Praise to His Name!

Chapter 5

The Mad Man -
The Key to the City

Between 2005 and 2006 the Lord raised an army in Northern Uganda from ashes to glory. An army, armed and dangerous, not with conventional weapons, but rather with the Word of God. It is this Word and its power which expanded and transformed this land in a miraculous, glorious way by raising the Acholi people from satanic bondage to heavenly freedom.

As Amos says, 'there has been a famine in the land for the hearing of the Word of God'. We could clearly see it in the faces of thousands in the camps as they asked for a Bible more than for a meal. Because they were not just physically hungry, but craved spiritual food even more.

When God said, 'Go north and just turn the light on, for light dispels darkness' that is what we did. His Word is the living light shining in the midst of the darkest corners by dispelling deception with the power of Truth. His Word is the very seed that sets men free and transforms the minds of those who are hungry for it. The hearing and reading of it brings light and understanding in the eyes and hearts of those who accept its truth. They are 'enlightened to see what is the hope of their calling!' And this is what began happening in camp after camp.

When word went out 'Bibles are here!', pastors were riding for hours on bicycles to come and pick up Bibles and take them to their villages. Not only that, they sat through our training classes which taught them how to conduct Bible study groups in the camps and begin prayer chains within their homes and churches. It was not long until they came back with reports of the fruit of these study groups, and of effective prayer chains, both

49

leading to countless salvations. The fertile ground of hearts was more than ready for planting a rich harvest of souls.

At the Favor of God ministry compound, the Saturday children's program had begun with 370 children on the first day, studying the Word, learning scripture songs, and being able to laugh again and enjoy games, sports and drama. Thank God for the healing power of His Spirit and the atmosphere of love that was able to restore years that the locusts had eaten. Without this hope, where would they be? As these day programs continued, we saw hundreds saved, receiving love, and have their little torn hearts mended within the arms of the most caring and compassionate heavenly Father.

The Bible College was in session and the response had been powerful. Most of the students were pastors from the towns or the camps in the area. They came, eager to be trained in the truths of the Heavenly Kingdom and to be 'thoroughly equipped for every good work'. Because the war had kept people back from finishing an education, most of these committed and faithful servants had never had the opportunity to even finish high school. But now they were able to sit and learn the Word, and even learn to read at the same time.

As Philip asked the eunuch, "Do you understand what you are reading?" and the eunuch said, "How can I, unless someone guides me?" (Acts 8:30- 31) This is what these men of God were being equipped to do, to guide others into all truth. It would be the Bible school students along with the pastors on the ground that turned out to be the team members for the portable Bible schools which began in the camps by the first part of 2006. Much prayer went up for this immense undertaking.

To continue the work, we needed visionary partners, ready to 'redeem the time' in the midst of war to see tables spread in the wilderness so that God's Kingdom might increase and multiply. That His people will 'rule in the midst of their enemies' and 'possess their gates' as He promises.

There was no doubt in anyone's mind, we had only a small window of opportunity left before the camps dispersed and people would be returning to their villages where they would be much harder to reach. This was the cry of urgency in my heart and that of the team for the almost two million Acholi people. We knew it would take an effort for 'all hands-on deck' in the Body of Christ, locally and abroad, to see this fulfilled in the short time we had left! "Oh Lord, revive your work in the midst of the years!" (Hab. 3:2)

Of course, we realized, there was no way Favor of God ministry could have any far-reaching impact other than in the area of Gulu without the Lord's divine intervention. Our hearts yearned to reach all of Northern Uganda before this window of opportunity would close. We beseeched the Lord to send His powerful Holy Spirit to fall in a mighty way for such a seemingly impossible vision to come about. But even with our strong faith and continued prayer, no one could have imagined how our mighty God began to bring this about in the most unexpected and unlikely way.

It was December 2005.

God's Word is NOT bound!! And neither is it threatened! It was one man God used to change the land in an astounding, dramatic way no one could have foreseen. His name was Awire and He was the strong man of Gulu, enslaved by the power of the enemy.

It all began one day as I prayed and God spoke clearly to me,

"The strong man in Gulu needs to be bound. All the satanic forces in this area are wrapped up in him. If he turns to Me, My power will break open the city."

I was stunned.

"Are you sure you know who you are talking about, Lord?"

Awire was a landmark in the city, well known and feared among the people. He was considered an insane lunatic with dreadlocks hanging down to his waist, which is a sign of occult involvement in Africa. These were matted with filth and feces and had not been cleaned in years. His fingernails were unusually long and also filled with feces. He ate only garbage from the garbage piles he slept on. His mind had been destroyed when his skull was fractured by the rebels several years ago. He was addicted to heavy drugs as he roamed the city streets naked, attacking many people violently at random.

Severely mentally disabled people like Awire have no place to go and are usually tied to a tree outside the village if they are a danger to society. These poor, tortured souls are then taunted, spit upon and poked at by passersby. Only a few take scraps or throw food for them from a safe distance.

Yet in spite of his violent, aggressive behavior, no one dared restrain Awire. Once, the government took him and sent him to Kampala, a six-hour drive away, from which he escaped and returned naked and on foot after running the entire way back to Gulu.

When I shared what the Lord had said to me with my team of thirty, they listened quietly.

"When God binds this man, we are going to see satanic goods spoiled," I said. "We will have a week of prayer and fasting and waiting for God to show up," I continued. In spite of this strange request, I did not sense any doubt on their faces as they left. Instead, two mornings later, into our week of prayer, I was awakened by a phone call at two o'clock in the morning. An excited voice on the other end shouted, "We got him, we got him!"

"What are you talking about?" I asked, trying to wake up from a deep sleep.

"We captured Awire!"

"What happened?"

"We knew where he was and went and restrained him and then prayed for the demons to leave him in the Name of Jesus. After he calmed down, we bathed him, cut his hair and put fresh clothes on him. He is very calm now and wants to come to the House of Prayer.

When they arrived, I could not believe my eyes. Awire was like a different man, not just on the outside, but his demeanor was calm, almost serene. It was still evident, his brain had been damaged by the skull fracture, but all the wildness and lunacy was gone. He allowed us to pray and minister to him without objection and with great calm over the next few days.

Word about his healing spread like wildfire across the town and the villages. As a result, our little House of Prayer was surrounded by hundreds of people from villages all around, who had brought their mentally ill. We prayed for each and every one and the Lord set them free, displaying the power of God and His Word in a mighty way. Even government officials came, together with hundreds of pastors from far and wide to see for themselves what had happened.

It proved Awire's story was instrumental in the defeat of the demonic stronghold in the area in and around Gulu and as a new level of faith and hunger arose in the communities, it opened a floodgate of countless new ministries, Bible studies, prayer groups and churches all over Northern Uganda.

Testimonies and reports of miracles and salvations, healings and church multiplication began pouring back into our little mission house. Bibles were distributed by the thousands around camps and villages, which had been twenty years without the active circulation of God's Word.

The team in Gulu would read these reports and declare, "Can you believe this? Blind eyes are being opened. Malaria is being healed. People are coming to Jesus right and left in the camps and villages and Bible study groups are popping up all over the place. All this is happening, just as the scriptures are read aloud in one village after another, with people sitting around the camp fires and one literate person reading for the other non-literates. It is as if the book of Acts has come alive."

"But why should we be surprised?" I told them. "Doesn't Romans 1:16 say that God's Word is the power of God for salvation, to all who believe?"

We now began to expect greater and greater things from the Bibles which were distributed into every home and village all over the north. After only a few years, we saw 50,000 Bibles given out freely. Since then, more than 60,000 Bibles in over 12 different languages have been the 'light turned on, dispelling darkness'!

As time went on, I kept hearing the Lord say, "Go take another camp. The land is yours. I've given it to you. I told you to ask me for the nations as your inheritance and the uttermost parts of the earth as your possession. You've asked me for it, now go take it! My Kingdom suffered violence, take it by force. There are giants in the land, but this is the promised land you've asked Me for. It's flowing with milk and honey and a large amount of fruit. The fruit is the greatness of the harvest you see coming in. The milk and honey is the sweetness of my presence doing it all, 'not by might, not by power, but by my Spirit'. The milk is the richness of my Word you are pouring out onto all those coming into the Kingdom. The giants are the obstacles such as sickness, money shortage, dangers on the road, loneliness and hardships of every kind. But know, they are like 'bugs' under your feet, and they will be crushed (Rom. 16:20) if you will keep walking forward. Wherever you set your feet, I will give you the land. Those who have never heard MUST hear. My own Father's Kingdom has suffered violence, and now only the violent will take it by force."

Awire stayed with us for five or six years, studying the Bible and slowly regaining his mental functions. He finally returned to his village, totally healed and farming his family's land. Such is the power of God, who touches those who seem lost in Satan's grip. For there is no power great enough to stand against our God, no purpose outside our reach if He declares it and every victory made possible if He ordains it. Because even in the remotest area of the earth, His love, power and dominion is made available through faith in His Word.

Chapter 6

Strange Fires in Anaka

My phone rang.

"Are you the leader of the House of Prayer?" a male voice asked.

"I am," I answered.

"Strange fires are falling out of the sky and they are burning huts and people and we don't know how to stop them." He sounded desperate. "Can your God help us?"

"Yes, He can," I answered with bold assurance. In my heart though, I had no idea what he was talking about or even knew whether to believe him or not.

"What do you want me to do?" I asked, a little stunned.

"Come to camp Anaka and I will show you."

I had gotten used to going into many unknown situations, never knowing what God had for me. Without hesitation I answered, "My God can help and I will come."

When I got to the camp, I met the chief in his 'office' which was located in a mud hut. He pointed to a stack of handwritten papers, "These are the reports from the last six months of fires falling from the skies. What makes them so strange is the fact that in spite of the huts in this camp standing so close to each other so the straw roofs touch, each fire only burns the one hut it falls on. As you know, usually if one of them catches fire, almost the entire camp burns down. This is all very strange."

He leaned toward me with a pleading look, wiping the sweat from his forehead in a tired gesture. "As you can imagine, the people here are terrified. Some children's clothing has burned. Thank goodness, none have been seriously hurt, but no one knows if their hut will be next. Each day, the people take all their possessions with them when they leave to dig in their gardens. We've closed our school down, since many of our children have unexplained grand mal seizures because of demon activities."

"When did all this start?" I asked, puzzled.

"It began when Joseph Kony and his soldiers came to the camp six months ago. His disciples, as they call themselves, gathered the children and sprinkled them with water, calling on the demons to anoint them and performing many animal sacrifices. Before they left, they demanded we turn over the most beautiful girl in the camp to them so they could sacrifice her on the altar of Satan. When we refused, they screamed at us and promised to unleash a thousand demons on the camp to spread darkness, terror and fear among the people." He sighed deeply, "And that is when the fires started." He looked at me with pleading eyes. "Can your God help us?"

"He can and He will," I answered again without hesitation, although I had no idea how God was going to do it. "I will return to Gulu and bring back some of my team to check out your stories first. At the same time, we will have many believers pray and fast for three weeks. After that, we will return after finding out what you say is true. I know our God will help if we ask Him." With that I left to return to Gulu.

I came back with twelve team members a few days later. In two by two's I sent them out to interview the people across the camp. They returned with identical tales of terror, fear and helplessness in the face of these fiery phenomena.

And then, it happened. As I was walking in the camp that very day, a flame fell from the sky and landed on one of the huts not far from where I stood. The place instantly burst into a raging bonfire. People came out shrieking in an unnatural, piercing way with some of their belongings in hand. Just as we were told, although the roof, made of dry straw, touched the next dwelling, it did not catch on fire. Since there was no water available, the affected hut burned into a heap of ashes within minutes. I tried to find signs of a source like a lighter, open fire or anything else, but could detect nothing which could have caused this. There was no doubt in my mind; we would have to return to help these poor people. I had never seen anything like this and knew this was the work of the enemy.

The occult practices and powers of the witch doctors in Africa are enormous. They hold a tremendous influence over the entire country, especially in the villages. These religious men are honored and revered for their powers, and in the absence of medical doctors, they perform healing rituals and incantations and help people in many other areas of life as well. They charge money for their services, and leave the people poverty stricken, with no help, and in deeper demonic bondage. Rarely do the people dare stand against them for fear of a curse being put on them, just as they had done in this camp. I knew our God would prove perfectly able to defeat the enemy and his demon forces once and for all if these witchdoctors would give their lives to Jesus.

For three weeks many people in Gulu fasted and prayed after I shared with them what was happening in Anaka. I assured them, God had given us power over every dark thing and authority over all demonic activity, no matter how strong they seemed to be.

I chose seventy believers who I knew to be great intercessors, plus some team members. We rented a truck and headed out to camp Anaka. I still had no strategy what to do once we got there, but then I never worried about that. The Holy Spirit would show us at the proper time.

On the first day after we arrived, I divided the people into several teams. One was to find the places where human and animal sacrifices had taken place. They were to pray over them and repent for the sins of the land and ask the Lord to cleanse it from the abominations committed there.

Another group was designated to go door to door and witness to people about Jesus, getting them to renounce the powers of Satan and accept Jesus into their hearts. It turned out, the people were so fearful of what had been happening, they took hold of the message of salvation eagerly, ready to trust the living God and turn their lives over to Him.

To another team, I gave instructions to find every one of the registered witch doctors in the camp and share the Gospel with them. Their assignment was to get them all saved.

Then I sent out several team members to find the children throughout the camp and invite them to participate in a kind of vacation Bible school, teaching them about Jesus and leading them into salvation.

Several people in our group spoke to the camp officials, sharing with them about the power of the living God who could defeat the power of Satan. So far, all they had ever known was demonic display, now they would see what God could do.

Each day at noon, we met under a big mango tree for prayer and music as crowds gathered to hear our message of salvation and how to be delivered from the bondage of the enemy.

On the second day, the monsoon rains started. It is not like regular rain, but an enormous downpour which lasts for about an hour each day. In spite of the rain, the flames began to fall again all over the camp.

"Satan, God will not be mocked!" I shouted in holy anger as I stood there, getting drenched under the mango tree. "You will not stop this meeting." I sent a group of prayer warriors to where the flames were falling. They took authority over the demonic activity and commanded it to stop. From that day on, not another flame ever fell again on the camp.

On the third day, we led hundreds of children, men and women to Jesus, breaking their covenant with demons that had been prayed over their lives from birth. We taught parents how to train their children in the ways and the Word of God, and we dedicated the land back to God.

But it was on the fourth day the big breakthrough came. I was preaching at an evangelistic public meeting under the mango tree in the evening, teaching the crowd how to pray to receive Christ. I then pointed out that they needed to pray for their children to be dedicated to the Lord instead of Satan. The witch doctors had sown animal hair, teeth or other strange items under the skin of the babies soon after they were born to signify their dedication to demons. While I was talking, a fourteen-year old girl rushed forward with her baby in her arms, crying out in a loud voice, "I want to give my baby to Jesus! I want to give my baby to Jesus!"

It was as if a dam had burst open and countless mamas came forward with their children, over two hundred in all. The team stood ready to break the many generational satanic curses over these precious children, to bless them as Jesus would, and to set them free. Hundreds of adults and children were saved that evening.

But God was not done yet. On the fifth day, the five witch doctors in the camp came and gave their lives to the Lord! Most of the camp officials were saved as well and the school was reopened. As the team taught them the truth of the power of God, children were prayed over and dedicated back to God, demonic covenants with the land and strange gods were repented of and renounced. It was a glorious time of salvation and deliverance as faith poured out on the camp that week.

One day, while a staff member was teaching, I was sitting in the first row of the crowd and a twelve-year old girl suddenly stood and walked towards me, her eyes blazing red and filled with hatred, while cursing at me in an unknown language. It was neither English, nor Acholi, nor any language I knew. As she reached where I sat, still cursing, I picked her up and motioned to the team leaders to help me. Suddenly, she struggled free and fell to the ground in a grand mal seizure, foam coming from her mouth and writhing in convulsions. Her strength was unbelievable and it took three men to carry her to a building nearby so we could minister to her.

Since it was evening, candles were brought to light up the room as men began to carry in more and more children, one after the other, who were shrieking and kicking violently. I knew the enemy was being stirred up beyond measure because these precious people were so ready to accept Jesus and be completely freed. The men began carrying the children, one by one, into our tiny prayer room that night, as the preaching continued out under the mango tree. We were tearing down the enemy's strongholds from every angle.

The men holding the children began hitting them when they couldn't get them under control.

"Don't hit them. Speak with authority in the Name of Jesus and cast out the demons," I shouted above the pandemonium. Then I told them, "Sing 'Oh, the blood of Jesus' and keep singing it over and over until we have ministered to all the children." They sang the simple song for six hours while the team members spent an hour with each child to cast out demons and break the demonic bondage. Between fifty and sixty children were set free by the time we stopped at two in the morning.

As children were prayed for, one after the other, they woke up as if from a coma and had no idea where they were. Their mothers came and held them close, singing over them and blessing them until they fell asleep. I instructed the parents in how to pray for them if they should show any signs of demonic torment again.

Within that month, we returned to the camp to begin discipleship training with a portable Bible school, which lasted two months. Out of which came the start of a church and many Bible studies and prayer groups. Word had spread rapidly throughout the northern regions of what God had done in Anaka! Once again, the Lord had used His miracle power to break through the darkness on a grand scale. What we could not have accomplished in many years, He did in a few weeks. Praise God!

A few months later, an official from the camp Patong called me with the familiar words, "Fires are falling on our camp. Can your God help us? We heard what He did in Anaka."

"Of course He can," I said with confidence. I was reminded of the verse that we overcome the enemy by the blood of the Lamb and the word of our testimony, and we love not our lives even unto death.

Instead of going myself, I contacted the new Christians in Anaka and sent them out to camp Patong to stand with the people there and push back the darkness, in the same way they had experienced. What rejoicing when the fires stopped and people were set free in the same way they had experienced before in their own camp.

Northern Uganda was not the same. God was on the move! But it was only the beginning of what He wanted to do in camp after camp, heart after heart, overflowing into the surrounding countries. Prayer movements were growing in the camps and villages, as people were taught the power of united prayer, voiced with purpose and direction from cleansed and repentant hearts. As they tasted and experienced the many answers, excitement was growing as greater hunger for prayer and the Word developed. "....times of refreshing are coming from the presence of the Lord....." (Acts 3:19). God was restoring the hearts of hurting people who had suffered for so long, drawing them into His Kingdom by the power of His healing grace!

In His goodness, God did not just bless the people, but Favor of God ministry as well. In the next two months, He increased our staff, who were gifted and anointed in specific areas. The Lord let us know that He was the one who drew them, to serve His people through this ministry on the ground. Some were gifted in accounting, some in working with children, and others in computer work and administration or in teaching. I knew without a doubt, HE truly was the Master Builder who said HE would build HIS church upon the rock and the gates of hell would not prevail against it! And that is what He did, using the hands of those who made themselves available to Him.

In Gulu, God provided another home with a large compound just for the children with thirty-three beds, including mattresses. But that was not all; the prison chaplain in Gulu came to my office one day.

"Mama Carole, we have had ministries come and go over time as we allowed them a week or a month for outreach within the prison. Your teams have been coming for several months now and the changes they brought are incredible."

I knew from reports and from going often myself, prisoners were being saved weekly. As they were released, they were going about testifying of the Lord's salvation, leading their families to Jesus and finding ways to serve their Savior.

"I beg you to add a women's ministry and let your teams do the same with them as they did for the men. Our doors are open to you until the Lord comes back!" he added with great emphasis. "Bring Bibles, as many as you can and keep on teaching the Word, because that transforms lives and sets the captives free, not just from prison, but from the grip of Satan.

We have come to realize the Gospel of Christ is what sets these men and women TRULY free!"

How I praised God for His faithfulness as I shook the man's hand and said, "We will do as you ask and allow God to bless this work. As you know, only He can bring the increase. We are just His instrument."

First Mission House in Gu

Carol teaching under a mango tree

Chapter 7

A Bride out of Ashes

God's presence was settling over the north in a powerful way because of the strength of united and consistent prayer. Word had spread far and wide about Favor of God and it seemed the book of Acts was coming alive as He continued to show His amazing power in ways almost too wonderful to believe. It began to be said of our team, 'these men who have turned the world upside down, have come here also.' (Acts 17:6)

The times of prayer at the Mission House were increasingly incredible! God was taking us into corporate worship as never before. He was leading us by His Spirit into the inner courts of communion with the heart of the Father, something the heart of God had longed to see. And in that place of worship, of waiting on Him and listening to the still small voice of His Spirit, He moved sovereignly, healing broken hearts, removing fear and torment, and restoring their souls, as He promised He would do.

Prayer and worship became the foundation of everything we did. It was the source of all ministry activities, the strategies He gave us for the land, the life style changes, war room planning sessions and the weeping room of intercession. We had prayer for two hours every morning, noon hour prayer and the Word downtown daily, all night prayers every Friday from 6 pm to 6 am, as well as a full day of prayer and fasting every Wednesday. Once every three months we began dedicating an entire week to prayer and fasting for the ministry, the land and its people. This became more than prayer, but a life style of hunger for more of Jesus for so many, who came daily, asking to be a part of what God was doing, because of the outpouring of miracles and His tangible presence.

I knew then God was shaking up not just northern Uganda, but also East Africa! I shared with the people that they had been self-consumed trying to survive and worrying how to find food from day to day during those many years of war. Now that peace had come, it was time to be vision bearers. I explained to them, a vision has to be bigger than they are and it has to involve serving the King through serving others. In other words, God must make leaders out of them. Because of the endless war, their culture had no core values like integrity, honesty, and character traits we get taught early on in most of our Judeo- Christian culture. I was actually attacked by community pastors, and even some of our team members, calling those core values witchcraft, manipulation and white man's culture.

"This is not American or African," I told them one day in a stern way, "this is Kingdom culture. You can leave if this is not what you want or you can stay and become men of God. The choice is yours. God does not change because you don't like what He says."

For the next five years I stayed in my little office room at the mission house, training and teaching these precious Acholi people to become leaders in the Kingdom and learn to do the actual work on the ground. Each day I sent them out and each day they would return with testimonies of God's miracles and blessings everywhere they went. I would send them out again and again, praying with them, training them, equipping them and then sending them forth in yet another direction.

I felt I was sent to unwrap their grave clothes and teach them to run free by helping to transform their souls and so bring transformation to all those receiving God's Word to whom they were sent. Only a transformed heart can transform a nation, and so they went.

HE proved the Faithful Shepherd who led us beside still waters to restore our minds, wills and souls and showed us that He can do, in a moment in His presence, what counseling cannot accomplish in a lifetime!

Jehovah Rapha was at work in a land which had been wounded and broken. Out of that brokenness, He raised a church that understood it takes suffering and self-denial to become true leaders and disciples of Jesus Christ.

He was raising up a glorious bride out of the ashes of the enemy's fire! He found her and plucked her from the fires of affliction in northern Uganda, called her out and gave her a new name. No longer called Forsaken or Desolate, but Hephzibah and Beulah, a land married to the Lord and rejoiced over by Jesus Himself, as a bridegroom rejoices over his bride. (Isa. 62:4-5)

How can I describe in human words the beautiful children in our home, once orphaned and abandoned, but now adopted by Jesus, singing to their Abba, Daddy, on their knees each night in the living room with their little hands and faces lifted towards heaven and their eyes closed, lost in the realm of worship? It was heartwarming to see them loving on their Father who healed their little hearts and gave them life and laughter once again.

How can I describe the visitation of God right into the prisons, tearing grave clothes and shackles off of bound up and destitute men and women and liberating them into a realm of freedom? Jesus, with skin on, walked into the prisons through obedient servants on the team and restored passion and purpose back into crushed and darkened hearts. As so many prisoners received Him into their lives every week, their cases were supernaturally dropped from higher courts. In turn, they were released and went into the community to serve their Savior and testify of His transforming power.

How can I describe the testimonies of those who had 'hungered and thirsted after righteousness' and God's Word for so long in the IDP camps? Now they were standing to give honor and glory to the Living God, who had not abandoned them, never forgotten them, and showed them His love by putting His Word into their hearts and into their hands. As they clasped the Bibles given to them, they testified of the powerful teaching of the Word, as they attended schools and training that 'opened the eyes of their understanding'.

How can I describe the radiance on the faces of the precious pastors and leaders all around the community, who came to feast at a table spread before them, rich with the power and encouragement of God's Word in the Bible schools, the retreats, and the training times? My heart leaped for joy as I listened to them give account again and again of how the entrance of His Word into their lives brought light and understanding and transformed their thinking, renewed their minds, and changed their lives and their ministries. Teaching, love and encouragement by our incredible staff over these servants of God in the community helped wash the dust of painful memories and weariness off the feet of these unsung heroes. They had walked through the kind of pain and suffering we will never know, see or begin to understand.

How can I describe the chorus of believers from the community and the camps, coming together at prayer and worship gatherings again and again, lifting hungry and desperate hearts to a loving Savior, who alone can forgive and heal a broken land? Through the heights of worship and the desperate heart cries of hungry children, God was no longer keeping silent. His heart was moved as His presence filled lives and filled rooms during these gatherings, all night prayer meetings, and even morning worship and devotion times at the House of Prayer. He healed physically, emotionally, mentally and spiritually what no human hands could have ever hoped to touch.

How can I share the depth of love and gratitude that overwhelmed my heart daily for the beautiful team and ministry staff God Himself had put together? He brought each one 'for such a time as this', and united hearts to truly move and work as one body. Their testimony and strength of that unity spoke volumes in a community shattered by division, death and civil war. What an awesome song of harmony rose from vision-filled lives as they shared, worked, loved, laughed and wept side by side, each one using his gifts and abilities to mend broken pieces of shattered lives and watched them become vessels of honor for the kingdom of God.

It is amazing how many doors He opened to reach out to the nation and its precious people. Following is a list of ministries the Lord raised up by the end of the year 2006.

NEW LIFE BIBLE COLLEGE

It had its first graduation of 20 students; 14 of whom were town pastors. A Bible College branch opened up in Lira, a neighboring district by February 2007. Within a few years, over 600 graduated from this two-year course.

BIBLE DISTRIBUTION

4,343 Acholi Bibles were distributed with Bible class training to pastors, church leaders, Sunday School teachers, prayer leaders, Bible school students, prisons and other local ministries. Sixty camps received Bibles, the main town of Gulu, and 5 districts in northern Uganda! Within a few years, over 60,000 Bibles were distributed in four nations and twelve languages.

PORTABLE BIBLE SCHOOLS IN THE IDP CAMPS

Seven two-month schools in seven camps took place that year, including children's camps, youth camps, prayer ministries, HIV prevention program, four crusades with the Jesus film being shown, two medical outreaches, children's conferences with sports evangelism, clothing distribution and military outreaches.

A total of 745 pastors and church leaders graduated from these training camps and 4,108 souls were saved during door to door evangelism, with follow-up! Within a few years, over 6,000 people have graduated from these bush training schools for pastors, with thousands upon thousands of souls saved.

LEADERSHIP TRAINING AND NETWORKING

Two pastors' retreats took place that year with books and resources given – 'Pastors Praying and Planning with Purpose'.

Two Leadership Training Conferences were held, and we oversaw the building of a church in one of the camps. We also had an electronic training class open to the community and a four-day worship conference. Within a few years, hundreds of pastors were helped in building and establishing churches, trained, given Bibles and resources and the Leadership Training Institute began.

HOUSES OF PRAYER

Houses of Prayer were established in ten IDP camps. Two three-day prayer gatherings were held in Anaka camp, two Schools of Prayer in the town of Gulu, and one night a month overnight prayer in the stadium reaching numerous camp and town pastors and prayer leaders. Within a few years, prayer movements and prayer gatherings in village after village sprung up all over the north.

HOUSE OF HOPE CHILDREN'S HOME

Our totally orphaned children came for permanent residence, with so many others, always waiting to move in. The home had a capacity for thirty-three children ages 1- 18. The staff consisted of 5 ladies, with 'father mentoring figures' assigned from the rest of our ministry staff. Within a few years, hundreds of community children had been helped in school, with medical needs, discipled in our youth outreach programs, and received an education through our work study programs.

FAVOR OF GOD PRIMARY SCHOOL

I didn't think we could run a school on top of everything else we were doing. But the call came from the government leaders again, "We've had so many years of war and no education. We need good schools where the Bible and character foundations are taught. Please, will you help us?" With staff in place that could open such a facility, we began, not because there were funds, but as always, just by faith.

You have to get out of the boat if you want to walk on the water. A few years later, we had over 400 children enrolled; some orphans, some Muslim children bringing their parents to Jesus, as they received Him at school. In a few years' time, we were named one of the best schools, academically and spiritually, in Gulu town.

PRISON MINISTRY

Men's and women's prison ministry ran two days a week, with 285 souls saved in the prisons that year and 61 attending a two-day Leadership Training within the prison. One hundred forty one Acholi Bibles were distributed plus English Bibles and other gifts. Within a few years, hundreds were saved in the prisons, with prison outreaches to the youth and vocational skills starting in the women's prison.

TRAUMA COUNSELING PROGRAMS

A Bible-based program for healing of the emotions in post war areas began in September of that year. Already four IDP camps and 576 people received the training, together with resource material. Many gave their lives to Jesus, and many more were healed of anger, nightmares, fear, torment and so many other wounds related to the trauma of the war. Within a few years, 40,000 had been through the two week trauma counseling program all over northern Uganda and 95% of them had given their lives to Jesus for the first time.

CHILDREN'S MAILBOX CLUB

This ten-week Bible study course for children was used in conjunction with Child Evangelism resources and was taught in the camps along with our portable Bible schools, as well as in the night commuter center in Gulu. A total of 2,694 children gave their lives to Jesus during these children's camps and 2,369 graduated from the 10 weeks of classes. Within a few years, kid's camps, and sports evangelism, along with the children's Bible study programs brought thousands more children to Jesus annually.

We were soon seeing it over and over again! Our Father started to transform hearts and minds as time went on, not just in our children, but with those who He sent to help us. Many who came to work with us and become our leaders in the ministry had been abducted as children and managed to escape the LRA. They were changed by the love of Jesus and changed from terrorists to peacemakers, from killers to vessels of healing and hope as well as Godly leaders. This happened not just once, but many times over as the Lord drew them to join us at the Favor of God team.

Latim, one of our leaders today, is one such man, whose testimony is amazing.

He was eight years old when he was abducted by the LRA and trained to be a child soldier. He served twelve years in guerilla warfare in unspeakably cruel and inhumane ways. He was trained in the use of AK47's and as a leader in mine placements in the bush of Sudan and northern Uganda, but I will let him tell his story in his own words.

"In 1992, when I was just eight years old, I was kidnapped by the LRA and taken to Sudan as a child soldier. They trained me to set land mines. I was ranked second best in our group. For a time, I was even taken as an attendant to help Kony and so was forced to do many things I never wanted to do, which are too cruel to share.

For twelve years, my life was always on the line and I was tormented by the darkness around me. However, God protected me even in this darkness. In 1996, I was sent with 31 other children into the battlefield, yet I was the only one who survived. In 1998, I had gone into the bush with five others to get food for the camp. We were ambushed as we went and I was the only one who returned. From this point onward, I started realizing there was a God who was watching over me. He did not just exist but He truly cared and loved me so much.

During 2000, the war was intense. We would begin fighting on the front lines at 10:00 am and finish at 3:00 am, firing bullets and hiding for 17 hours a day. On one of these days, a plane flew over us which, of course, meant bombs. The plane dropped a bomb right beside my hiding place. There was an anthill near and as the bomb hit the ground the soil from the hill buried me, leaving only my head above ground. I stayed in the bush in this state for three days. During those three days, enemy soldiers continued to walk directly beside where I lay. Praise be to God, He made me invisible and none of these soldiers saw me for the entire three days. It wasn't until the fourth day that some fellow soldiers walked by and found me buried in the dirt. For three days I hadn't had any water or food, but once again, God protected me and showed His love for me.

In 2003, I found out that my mum and dad had been burnt alive, inside of their house. When I heard this, it broke me inside. By this time, I had 5 wives and 8 children, but at this news, I made up my mind to go back home. My first wife told me, "We can't go. If we leave they will kill all of us." But I was adamant that I was going to pay my respects to my parents. If it meant dying then I would die and be with them.

We set out toward Uganda from Sudan and walked for three days without rest because we knew soldiers were pursuing us. There were 53 of us travelling together but we moved in smaller clusters for safety. When we reached Karuma, where the bridge crosses the Nile River, we were ambushed. Planes began to fly overhead showering bombs, and the soldiers who had been pursuing us now opened fire. One bomb exploded near me hitting my legs with shrapnel. The six others in my group died in this attack. I escaped only by covering myself with the body of a fallen friend and pretending to be dead. I lay there until some other soldiers found and rescued me. Later, I found that twenty others had been seriously injured. Upon rescue, our group was sent to the capital city of Kampala where we stayed for nearly two years. I never did return to my home village. Instead, in 2007, I went back to Gulu to try and find a way to support my family. My lack of education and skills were a serious barrier, but I began to pursue a driving course and that is how I first met Favor of God Ministries. This ministry has done so much in my life, changed me and turned me around that words cannot express or appreciate it all. I just thank God so much for Mum Carole, together with the team who are supporting her. May God bless them each so much. I don't have a father or a mother but God brought Mum Carole as a mother to me.

I gave my life to Jesus, through Favor of God, and then God has blessed me with my own land through the ministry's help. I have built some homes on my land, for my children, and the wonderful Christian wife that I married. I pray that God will take full control of my life to walk in all He wants me to do, and that I would not ever think about my days as a soldier and the things I did, but instead to focus on God's work alone."

Through Favor of God Ministry's love, discipleship and support, Latim now has a farming business and built his own houses on the land, where he can raise his children without fear of man, but in the fear of the Lord.

Latim's story is a perfect example of the life and suffering of the thousands of children, and even adults, who have lived a life of horror and violence. Those who were not abducted were controlled by daily fear of losing their lives or that they would be taken.

This is why the children's home became a haven of safety and security for those who made it there, and why the ministry became a family for those who had none. Broken hearts were mended and shattered minds restored.

God was bringing hope where there was hopelessness and love where there was hatred, so He could raise up an army of anointed warriors to bring peace to a people and a land that had been devastated by the power of hell through Satan's evil forces.

Through the lives of rescued children and delivered adults, He began to 'restore the years the locusts had eaten.' The Father's power was a marvelous thing to behold as He conquered the enemy, not with guns, but through the love of the Gospel. What a privilege to allow me to be a part of this gradual transformation of a people given up for dead.

God had opened the floodgates of heaven over the land of Northern Uganda to a measure no human hand could possibly have accomplished because of united, continued prayer. He is a great and mighty God and He did great and mighty things in a broken, hurt and devastated land with a people raised from the ashes of total destruction. I stand in awe at His power, goodness and mercy in the face of such revival to this day.

However, all this came at a price. In the midst of this frantic pace, which brought physical and mental exhaustion, I felt a crushing loneliness and even despair. There was no one I could turn to and share; no one to open up my heart about my feelings of doubt, fear, and depression. Not because I doubted God could do it, but wondering if I could, because of the many mistakes I made along the way. After all, this was a different culture, a different set of values, void of honesty, integrity and decency. I was alone, a woman in a man's world. And a lot of these men preyed on me for money, partnership in the ministry and finding a way to get to America through me.

I realized I lacked the discernment of their true motives and had to learn the hard way not to trust their words. I cried out to God, "Please teach me the true motives of men!" I cried out at night as I lay weeping on my bed each time I failed.

It is hard for me to find the words to describe the stark loneliness I felt in those days. I felt so helpless against the needs around me constantly. I felt I ministered and gave out of brokenness and loneliness but He was always faithful to pour out of my broken places onto the needs of others.

In all of my failings and shortcomings, I experienced His grace beyond measure, as Jesus took each failure and washed it away with His blood, teaching me to forgive, trust, and lean harder on His loving guidance. His immense love and forgiveness was the light which guided me through the darkness of those days.

I had only one friend, but she lived in another town. There was no way I could share with any of the Acholi women about these feelings. It was so ingrained in them not to show emotions that my sharing would have been impossible for them to grasp. Neither could they have kept what I told them confidential.

Because of my exhaustion, the depth of my despair was sometimes like a dark hole of death around me. Yet it was this death that brought light and life to others as the Lord proved faithful and brought me joy with each new day. He showed me that in my own weakness, it could only be God doing what He was doing, in Northern Uganda, through HIS power and righteousness, not mine.

It was during this dark time, after a long, hard day, I felt tired and exhausted, ready to sink into bed. There was a knock on the door. It was one of the team leaders from a portable Bible school in the North-East.

"I have to tell you a story, I just have to," he shouted.

I waved for him to come in.

"I was mobilizing for a new Bible class when they brought an insane man to me, biting, kicking and totally out of his mind. He had been chained to a tree for a long time and was in an agitated state as he stood before us. We prayed for him and the Lord set him free and healed him." He was shouting again. "Mama Carole, we washed him and gave him fresh clothes and fed him and he was completely normal. Not only that, he was the first to show up for the Bible class the next morning and hasn't missed a lesson since."

"Isn't it just like our God to pick the leftovers, the people no one wants and gives up for trash and turns them into His beloved children?" I said with rejoicing. I had experienced many of these stories and yet they never failed to touch my heart with the compassion and goodness of an almighty God, who gathered His Bride out of the ashes. One more testimony made it worth it all.

That night, I opened my journal to read a poem I had written years ago. It describes best how I found I could trust in His comfort and love, certain that He would always raise me up from any discouragement or despair.

I KNOW YOU'RE THERE

Lord, through a valley of deep despair,
I've got to know you're always there.
I need to know I'm not alone,
When my heart seems miles away
from home.

When I've stumbled through endless,
wakeful nights,
When my soul is gripped with sorrow
or fright,
When my heart has fallen to the depths
of despair,
Then Jesus, just let me know you're
there.

Reach out a hand through the
darkening cloud,
And to my yearning soul, whisper
aloud.
And there in that darkness, just by
your grace,
Focus my eyes on Jesus' face.

Let me see the light of His tender
smile,
Telling me night will be worthwhile,
For after each night, there comes a
new day,
When rays of hope take darkness
away.

The sun comes up, He shows me the
light,
For victory has dried the tears of the
night.
Then I'll see how my faith was built up
strong,
And I'll start the new day with another
song.

Without a night, there could be no

Sometimes it's hard to hear His call,
When the darkness of night begins
to fall.
It's hard to see He's waiting with
grace,
When the tears have clouded,
streaming my face.

I know He's there, I must believe,
By faith His presence I receive,
Yet feelings are such a part of me,
They're hard to forget so passively.

I need to learn more than ever
before,
That I can never have any more,
Till I yield the feelings that have me
bound,
And step by faith onto higher
ground.

Teach me Lord what's hardest to
learn,
How my heart does ache and deeply
yearn,
For when I've wanted to do my best,
I've fallen short of your perfect rest.

Jesus, you know, and you deeply
care,
You know more than I what's really
despair,
You know what it's like to really
give,
You know the secret of how to live.

It was hiding in God, abiding there,
Sheltered from burdens you
shouldn't bear,
And there, wrapped up in His
covering wing,

Send Me Where No One Wants to Go

dawn,
And without trials, faith wouldn't be strong.
And without fire which burns away dross,
Impure gold would be counted a loss.

If there was sunshine, but never the rain,
If there was joy, but never the pain,
I'd never know what my faith could do,
And I'd never learn how to lean on you.

I thank you Lord for the darkest night,
For even the valleys have a ray of light.
Cause it's you, dear Jesus, just being there,
Just keeping your promise and showing you care.

Even through darkness and loneliness,
When my heart is nothing but emptiness,
Whether or not I'm really aware,
My dear Lord Jesus is standing there.

He's calling to me with a longing deep,
To shelter and cradle His wandering sheep,
To hold me close to His yearning heart,
No longer alone, standing apart.

You learned how to fight, you learned how to sing.

Jesus, take me by your grace,
Take me to your hiding place,
And as I stand wrapped up in Thee,
The enemy comes, but has to flee.

And teach me Lord, abiding in you
Is longing to do what you would do,
To release all guilt because you forgive,
To live IN YOU when it's hardest to live.

If I can learn from every mistake,
From heartaches and wounds, the beauty you make,
I'll see the night is worth each tear,
And the light of the dawn finds You ever near.

Chapter 8

Taking the Kingdom by Force

July 2007 marked Favor of God's second birthday and, as we went into our third year, we looked back and praised our Mighty God for all He had done for us, in us and through us. We also looked toward the future fulfillment of the dreams and visions He had given us to help bring transformation to northern Uganda…one life at a time and one day at a time.

He used the Empower Program, a Trauma Counseling (TC) method developed by Dr. Robi, from Australia. Favor of God Ministries was the first to implement this ground-breaking program in an effort to bring emotional and spiritual help and healing to the war-torn Acholi people.

Eventually, we were able to help 3,000 people face and deal with traumatic and stressful life-events in more than 12 camps. Over the next five years, over 40,000 people went through the program. Of those, 95% accepted Christ as their Savior. This program and its message, using the application of the scriptural principle of forgiveness, had a powerful effect on those who took the course. There are so many stories of wounds healed and broken lives made whole, it is hard to share just a few. Each camp had its different stories and even we, the workers, have our own experiences of how "Empower", as we called it, changed our lives to where we will never be the same!

Imagine, during the past twenty-one years, northern Uganda experienced the ravages of civil war, leaving thousands of people homeless; many without relatives and with only the clothes on their backs. Eighty five percent of the population of northern Uganda had been forced to move into IDP camps after their homes were looted and burned. Most of them experienced unimaginable horror and hardships and the loss of loved ones through the most brutal assaults. Empower helped them face these events, and the feelings attached to them, work through forgiveness, and gave them hope and a future once again.

A great number of the people we trained were abducted soldiers of the rebel group, the Lord's Resistance Army (LRA). They had witnessed or been involved in the murder of close family members, seeing all their food and possessions stolen. Yet when they went through this course, almost all found forgiveness and peace and came away with a great desire to help others, as they had been helped.

This two-week program was divided into two parts. The first helped the person face his or her traumatic event(s) in a calm manner by learning to deal with these situations by facing stressful or traumatic situations in a manner which did not bring more stress or trauma. The next part, presented the concepts of forgiveness, referring to the Bible and the examples of Jesus. So many of the participants found faith in Jesus and decided to follow Him, bringing a new lifestyle of peace and wholeness. They received forgiveness, in order to give forgiveness, towards themselves and others.

Ojara, who later became the man in charge of our twelve trauma counseling teams, arrived at my office one day and said,

"Mama, are you the crazy, white lady? I know you reach and change people and I want to do the same." He sounded and acted very sure of himself. "I just finished my university degree in Kampala and want to bring healing and hope to this land, too."

"I am very proud of you finishing your education and your degree, Ojara. Unfortunately, that doesn't matter much in the Kingdom of God. I care much more about how it stands with your heart, your character and how you walk with Jesus," I answered.

"With my education, I am worth a lot of money," he added, unfazed by what I had said.

"We do not pay you in money if you want to work here. We can give you a place to stay and food." I pointed to Achang, who was outside in the yard cooking. "You see that lady out there," I asked, "she makes $12 a month. You can make that if you want a job with us."

"I didn't go to school for nothing. I am better than that!" He was shouting angrily. "I want you to know, I paid for that education and I am not settling for a mere woman's wage." With that he turned and left.

The next day he came back, looking a lot less arrogant.

"You know about that position I talked to you about yesterday? I want it. I have decided I want to serve the King and my people and I will take whatever Achang makes."

Ojara proved to be a gifted man with quite a temper. When he shouted at Achang one day that he would not take orders from a woman, I stopped him and said, "I am a woman. We are all the same in God's eyes."

The next day he asked for forgiveness, again. And so it went for quite some time, yet he always came back, repenting and willing to submit and learn. "God can use anyone that is teachable," I would always remind him. "Always be willing to stay humble."

Ojara became a true leader of leaders, teaching the trauma counselors because of his teachable spirit and submitting not only to God, but to the authority God had placed over him. Here are some of the stories he tells of how the counseling program changed lives in the many villages he ministered in the area.

A woman, whose husband was missing after an enemy raid, had worked very hard to produce food for herself and her 6 children. One night, while she and her children were sleeping in their home, she dreamed the government soldiers were coming. By the time she woke up, the rebels had surrounded her home and were kicking in the door. First, they tortured her, all the time threatening to kill her. They abducted her and her last-born child, who was just learning to talk, leaving her other five children behind. The soldiers dragged her along with them and made her witness the murder of many people and constantly threatened to kill her as they marched throughout the night. When they met up with other rebel troops, she was ordered to cook food for them, but she, herself, was not given anything to eat. For three nights, the rebels and their captives marched farther into the bush until they reached a very remote, mountainous area near Sudan.

During this time, she had no idea what had happened to her other children at home. Her feet swelled severely but she knew the rebels would kill her if she stopped walking. They finally reached a cave where they stored their supplies and provisions and made camp. What they didn't know was that the government soldiers had laid an ambush for them there and started firing.

The woman ran as the rebel leader attempted to stop her. The child on her back kept shouting, "Run away, Mommy, run away!" As she continued to flee, bombs began falling and her captors scattered, running for their lives. Many people were killed all around her. She tried to escape across a swamp and fell into the water with her child. They survived but were confronted on the other side by the rebel leader again. He jeered at her and called her a wicked lady. She continued to run. When she finally stopped to rest, she found herself on another mountain, alone with her child and not knowing how to get home. After traveling with the rebels for three days, she had lost all sense of direction. Just as despair began to take hold of her, she saw a young man from her village who had been among the twenty people who had been abducted from her area.

They stayed together and began walking on foot and soon met two other women who joined them. The young man from the village became their leader. They moved until night and slept in the forest with no shelter from the heavy rains. As they walked on, looking for some familiar landmarks, they found bananas and raw cassava to eat – a feast after being without food for over three days of hard marching. Finally, the young man recognized a place where he used to go hunting and then knew where they were. From there he led his little band home. Her children and relatives had heard that she had been killed, so the rejoicing was loud and long when they saw her and her young child walking into the village.

But her emotions seemed to have died. She couldn't cry or feel anything and said, "I am just a woman without a husband, trying to take care of my children. The rebels took everything I owned. I have nothing left." She locked herself in her home and cried for hours. She did the same thing the next day until another woman came and said, "I'm going to destroy your door if you don't open." When she finally did, the woman said to her, "Isn't life worth more than these material things? All your children are still alive."

That is when she decided to attend the TC program, which was soon to be presented in her area. At the end of the "Empower" sessions, she gave her life to Jesus Christ and found a new life of forgiveness and peace. Such is the healing power of the love of Jesus! He can heal the wounds and even erase the painful memories.

Another story that remains clearly in my mind is that of a lady who had experienced trauma from both the rebels and the government soldiers. At that time, the government was emphasizing that all people must go to the camps, so she and her family went. But the rebels came into the camp, abducted many people and killed her husband. This lady's brothers came a few days later and went to report the attack to the government. While on their way, the soldiers killed them. She was filled with hate and fury every time she caught sight of any army men. Finally, she decided to go through the TC program which was coming to her camp. During the program, she came to a place where she could forgive the soldiers and the rebels who had killed her loved ones and she received forgiveness for herself through faith in Jesus Christ. The rage and hate left her and she was able to raise her children in a healthy environment.

During the counseling sessions, many of the participants asked, "Where was God when this happened to me? How could He allow such horror and cruelty?" We gently shared Deuteronomy 30:15-20 at such times.

Others told us, God couldn't possibly understand how they feel. We shared Hebrews 4:15 and Isaiah 51:3 with them. Still others asked if it was really possible to forgive and go on with life. With them we shared Romans 8:26-28.

One woman in the camp, who had not yet come to the class, had lost all of her children during a massacre that was led by the second in command of the LRA; a man whom she knew. The rebels entered the village school and killed all the children. Some months later they returned and massacred many adults in that same village. This forced the survivors into an IDP camp. The woman told us she could not forgive the rebels. We continued to pray for her, knowing one day, God would give her a testimony of the power of love and forgiveness through salvation in Jesus Christ. And that is just what Jesus did.

Two more women shared their stories.

"One day, at about 5:00 in the morning, government soldiers reached my home when all my children were asleep. Four of my children were taken by them, and as they moved a short distance from my home, they clubbed them all to death and piled their bodies together in a heap. In the morning, I tried following them to see where they could have gone and I met one of the soldiers who directed me to the scene. When I saw the sight of the bodies of my babies, I collapsed. Later, a man from the village helped me bury my children. The hatred in my heart towards these men was unbearable, but now, as I received Jesus into my heart in this program, I am able to forgive the soldiers."

"I am a seventeen-year-old girl," another woman shared. I was abducted at the age of thirteen and stayed in the bush for a year. I remember one day, when one abductee, who tried to escape, was caught and I was ordered to kill her, but I could not. Instead, she was given to a boy who cut off her head with a panga knife right in front of me. After that, I was almost beaten to death for disobeying orders and refusing to kill her. I remained in a coma for a long time, but I did not die. They refused to treat me as part of my punishment and it took three months to recover. One day we encountered a government soldiers' ambush and that is how I escaped and returned home. And now I am coming to this program, wanting to learn about the love and forgiveness of Jesus."

Listening to these many horrible stories helped me to forget about myself and my problems. It made me appreciate my own life and my desire to help others was strengthened. It was God's grace alone that healed broken lives and drew so many to Him, touching one life at a time with His healing love.

One of the primary goals of Empower was to encourage the participants to share with others what they received from the program. They, more than any of us, could help their families, friends and communities deal with terrible traumatic situations in their past, and see the healing power of Jesus flow through them, just as they themselves had experienced.

We supported a long-term economic rehabilitation system for the people of northern Uganda. This helped promote and support community-based income generating activities that were sustainable without outside financial support.

The Favor of God Mission House was the hub of all ministry activities. The house became well known in both the community and the camps as a haven and landmark of God's presence. Many times, individuals and even whole families came, unbidden, asking how to be born-again. The office, located behind the house, contained administrative offices for the staff of over twenty by now, as well as a community library and resource center and a center for Bible distribution.

It was our goal to build altars of prayer in every village across northern Uganda, as well as southern Sudan. We desired to see the Church of the Sudan (southern Sudan and northern Uganda) united in prayer and purpose as the Gospel was preached to every soul. How we praised our Mighty God for all He did here in northern Uganda through Favor of God Ministries. We especially thanked Him for the faithful partners He brought here, in body and/or in spirit, to work beside us in these white and ready harvest fields. This included those in the United States, who had given so generously. Today, we can all stand hand-in-hand and heart-to-heart, praising Him together and saying, "Look what God has done!"

Our House of Hope Children's Home leaders, worked tirelessly to see our children loved, healed and given a stable family environment in which to develop their identities as children of God. We strongly believed God would take these precious 'victims of war' and turn them into 'instruments of revival'. We set out to diligently instill in them the Biblical principles of character, ethics, morality, integrity, and Godly core values that would mold them into becoming strong future leaders for this country.

Many churches and community leaders all over Northern Uganda began to request additional ministries and services, which led to much prayer on the part of the Favor of God leadership and staff. As a result of this prayer, the ministries we ran were birthed.

One day in our morning devotions, I said to our leadership team, 75% of who were men, "Get pregnant with vision, and let it enlarge you. Then go to the weeping room of intercession, with a passion for souls too deep for you to contain, and begin travailing to give birth, as Isaiah 66 says. When you give birth to something, you will die for it. Take ownership of God's work, and let it propel you with a zeal that consumes you, as you look daily upon the face of the Father, and then into lands, that are afar off, yearning to know Him." (Isaiah 33:17)

From this challenge, and within the heart of our own leaders, a prison ministry, which consisted of evangelism and Bible school to prisoners in both the men's and women's prisons, was birthed. Hundreds of men and women gave their lives to Jesus and were trained up in leadership development within the prison, so they were ready to run as missionaries, as soon as they were released.

We took Bible studies to the schools and the University in town, to the campuses, and to the communities. The Word spread like wild fire into the military barracks, and after sports events with the soldiers, we would give them Bibles each week. They

studied the Word, and took them along into countries like
Somalia, and Sudan, Rwanda, and Congo.

Training retreats were being held every two months for
pastors and church leaders throughout northern Uganda. These
were times of refreshing for worn and weary leaders, who would
come for a good meal, hear an encouraging word, receive more
Bibles and children's material for their churches, pick up our
love offering for their church repairs, and allow us to wash their
feet for the paths of ministry ahead of them.

The IDP camps took years to disband as people slowly
began moving home to their own land, after 20 years of war. We
became the 'help center' for any urgent needs or emergencies, as
the community realized the Father's love that flowed through our
team to every person and situation alike. We distributed clothing
and started medical and dental outreaches where these had been
absent for 2 decades. But in all of our doing, the Gospel was
going. It must be Jesus first. Preach Him, teach Him and then
feed them. Did God call His church to educate demons and put
band aids on devils and leave them that way? Of course not.
What good was medical help, food, education and clothing if we
were going to leave them spiritually unchanged, facing an
eternity of hell?

Three-day prayer, teaching and evangelistic crusades, using
the Jesus Film, were conducted in camp after camp, followed
with salvation, praying for the sick, and seeing God save, heal,
and deliver hundreds from demonic oppression, every single
time. The growth of new believers began to enlarge the little
village churches, and as more and more students were graduating
from our Bible schools, they would establish new church plants.
The body of Christ was exploding with multiplication, at a rate
faster than we could count or even document.

Classes were held twice weekly at the Mission House to
train believers in personal and corporate Bible study methods.
Each participant received a Bible in his/her own language and
committed to start a Bible study group or a Sunday school class
in their own village, as they took five Bibles home to distribute

there. They were expected to submit an accountability report on their Bible groups that were started. We began teaching them in a poverty stricken land, that God still holds us accountable. The Word of God is free, but not cheap. It cost Jesus everything. Now go and freely give, as you have freely received. That is exactly what they did.

The Lord, who had raised His Bride out of the ashes of destruction, continued to adorn her with such abundance of restoration and spiritual blessings, it made us stand in awe at His love and miraculous power. The land that was forgotten by the world had become the apple of His eyes in just a few short years. Just as spoken in Zechariah, 'I will remove the sin of the land, in a day', that is what we were witnessing. Only the blood of Jesus could cleanse and heal, forgive and restore, as we were watching Him do. I give Him all the praise and the glory!

"From the days of John the Baptist until now, the Kingdom of heaven has been forcefully advancing, and forceful men lay hold of it." Matthew 11:12

Chapter 9

Still a General, but in God's Army

During these years of explosive growth, between 2007 and 2009, this became our favorite battle cry. I remember my daughter writing to me one day, "If God uses you so much when you have been emotionally crippled, just think of what He could do with you if you were whole." This really stuck with me and I realized, if we wanted to take the Kingdom by violent force in Northern Uganda, there would have to be a continual deep and desperate spiritual, physical and emotional healing in the leadership. God doesn't send wounded warriors into battle.

Almost every staff member had come from a traumatic background, and had to walk daily through the steps of forgiveness, deliverance, learning to remain in the love of Jesus. Only through this violent, all overpowering love and His power, could they take the land and change the hearts of the people. Could God really build the plane in the air while it was flying? It seemed to be just what He was doing with our team - and still does. He used us to build His church, even though we were still under construction!

I want to share with you the story of one such member of our team. His name is Ochan. He was an officer in the Ugandan government forces for twenty years, trained as a fighter pilot in Israel, until the day he was captured by Kony's rebels. For many months in the bush, he endured the most horrible torture, brain washing, being forced to participate in occult practices like drinking human blood, killing, maiming and raping countless victims. Finally, his soul and conscience died and he succumbed to the demonic influences to such an extent, he became one of Kony's general leaders for the next twenty years. During this time, he watched the extreme power of Satan in action as he witnessed and participated in thousands of executions, tortures, massacres; all to the dedication and enslaving power of the demonic authority he was serving under.

When the government forces finally captured him back from the LRA rebel group twenty years later, his mind was in torment and filled with horrific darkness. By now, in his sixties, he was released by the government to seek retirement. He came to Gulu and stopped at an open-door crusade. It was here, under deep conviction, he accepted Jesus as his Savior. He immediately came to the House of Prayer for discipleship, and from then on never missed a prayer meeting. His life was totally transformed after he was prayed over for deliverance many times and was gradually able to forgive his captors. During these sessions, he would tell us of some of the things he experienced while working close to Kony.

"Kony would pray and fast often to keep his powers," Ochan shared. "He spent many days fasting and pleading with Satan not to take the power from him."

Then one day, as he was sharing some of his experiences, Ochan asked me, "Tell me the exact time you led the first stadium prayer in Gulu." When I told him he probed further, "What month and what week was that?" When I told him, he said, "That is the exact time Kony came to me and told me the power had left him."

In awe and wonder we realized, the enemy has to flee and Satan's power must be broken when the church begins to pray! We also understood this was the 'violence' Jesus was talking about when He told us to take the Kingdom of God by force. He meant the force of His power in pushing back spiritual darkness, and bringing His presence in to heal the land. His love was the same force which changed every heart.

Ochan became one of our most fervent and powerful intercessors and taught us much about spiritual warfare. After all, he had first-hand experience in serving the devil and his forces for twenty years.

One outreach took us to the village of Patong, where we were going to pray for the land to see it redeemed back to the Kingdom of God by leading people to Jesus. As we traveled around that region, Ochan led our team to pray and push back spiritual darkness in specific places, where animal sacrifices had taken place. We witnessed to the witch doctors, who gave their lives to Jesus, and saw hundreds of souls of the villagers come to salvation. As violent as Ochan had been when fighting for the kingdom of darkness, he was equally as violent driving it out on behalf of the Kingdom of God. Imagine, the Lord had sent us a general to prepare the way!

The fruit of harvest was overwhelming in Patong during those weeks. As more of our ministry team members came to join us on the field, the spiritual ground had been prepared for harvest. We held town meetings, door to door evangelism, held Bible studies, church services and Bible clubs for children. This went on in village after village, town after town for weeks on end. The Lord was turning the world of Northern Uganda around, freeing His bride from the clutches of darkness, turning on the light of Jesus in one heart after another. In many villages, we were able to plant churches or strengthen the small ones we found there already, amazed at the unbelievable outpouring of blessings and presence of Jesus in the entire region.

It was after we witnessed many miracles and lives touched in Patong, our tired team was on the five-hour journey home. One of our leaders, who had been with us on that long and exciting mission, asked us to make an extra stop on the way back. We would be driving through the village where his father had just been hospitalized for drug overdose the day before in a small rural clinic.

Our staff leader had been praying for his family's conversion for years, and up to now, none of them had accepted the Jesus he so wholeheartedly served. His father, who had been struggling with long illnesses, discouragement, and hopelessness, had taken poison the day before to bring his despairing situation to an end. The poison had not killed him, however, because his son prayed so fervently for his father's salvation. Because, for a long time, he had stood faithfully in the gap for him to 'come into the Kingdom of light', the heavenly Father heard his heart-cry.

Our weary team drove up to the little village clinic, where we found the father on the bed, his wife and another son were also at the bedside. As our team shared with the family members present the love, the healing, and the grace of the Father's heart for each one of them, they all asked to receive Jesus into their hearts. With hands lifted, they prayed the salvation prayer, all giving their lives over to the only living God! And not only did his family receive Jesus, but two other patients who were sharing the same room, gave their lives to the Lord as they witnessed this precious scene. The Lord Jesus restored our leader's father to health, and he returned to his home with joy to start a brand-new life.

As we drove home that evening, there was great rejoicing and dancing with the angels in heaven, who dance over every life redeemed by Jesus. He came to seek and to save the lost (Matt. 18:11) and as the Father sent Him, so sends He us. (Jn.20:21) His harvest is ready to be gathered, waiting on us to obey!

Gulu means 'Heaven' in the Ugandan language, and we felt it had become heaven's gateway for God's glory to come and reign and blanketing northern Uganda. Spiritually, we felt positioned as a gateway for His Word and His power to flow across this land and northward. Geographically, we are located on the unseen line of the 10/40 window, the areas of northern Africa, most untouched by the Gospel.

Our inheritance is the glory Jesus receives and gives to His Father. Yes, there were giants, there were strongholds, and there was warfare in gaining the ground the Father had commissioned us to gain for His Kingdom. But it was also the land flowing with milk and honey. A land of fruitfulness, and great harvest for the Kingdom of heaven! And the enemy's oppositions were like grasshoppers before the army of the living God! One camp at a time, God gained the territory back through the hearts of believers who reached out to possess their inheritance! If Jesus said the harvest is ripe and ready now, as He did in John 4, then 'ripe' today means 'rotten' tomorrow if we don't reap.

One day, I said to our team,

"Smell your fist. If it doesn't smell like smoke, you're not living close enough to hell. Doesn't Jude 23 say, 'snatch them out of the fire'? This means, we better live close enough to the flames of eternal burning, to pull out the precious lives who have fallen in." We were a team that marched to heaven's drumbeat and lived with eternity in our hearts! On our mission house wall hung the statement of a great missionary man, "I'll go to hell and back to reach them, if you'll just hold the ropes." I was seeing God's army before me, men and women set apart for the Kingdom.

We were going after the lost with everything in us, opening their eyes, in order to turn them from darkness to light, away from the power of Satan to God, so they might receive forgiveness of sins and join us in the inheritance God had ordained for them. The Apostle Paul said, 'I was not disobedient to this heavenly vision.' (Acts 26:18-19), and neither were we!

In changing lives from one army to another, the Lord used His willing, worshipping warriors to reach one camp at a time, one village at a time and down to one soul at a time. He knew each of them by name and gathered them carefully and with great, tender love. But He did not leave them the way He found them; hurt, bruised and maimed physically and emotionally. In His army, the real battle ground was not fought with guns and rockets, but with the weapons of spiritual warfare, which are not carnal, but are mighty for the pulling down of strongholds. (II Corinthians 10:4) For we were not fighting against flesh and blood, but against the rulers, against the authorities, against the powers of darkness and the spiritual forces of evil in the heavenly realms. (Ephesians 6:12) With this in mind, we knew we were opposing an already defeated foe. (Colossians 2:15)

The preciousness of God's Word discovered for the first time.

Chapter 10

Midnight Wrestlers

To win this war, we did not use our own strength or power, but we fought on our knees and in the precious Name of Jesus, like Daniel, Jacob, Paul, Jesus, and so many others. It was His Name which not only put the enemy to flight, but through His Spirit of unconditional love and forgiveness, the countless victims of this terrible war were made whole to begin a new life and walk in a new destiny. The reward for our team was not measured in earthly riches, but in the many precious, restored lives of the people of Northern Uganda. How often we quoted the famous words of Jim Elliot, "He is no fool who gives what he cannot keep, to gain what he cannot lose."

Our personal motto became, 'Dreams are made in the dark, lonely prayer closets, when it's just you, God and the calling; believing in a vision with tangible promises and intangible evidence, until vision becomes reality.'

And from these secret prayers, God brought open results. There was an intense hunger, a deep desperation, a passionate pursuit, and an unquenchable thirst coming from the church in northern Uganda for the totality of God's heart. Our soul was longing, even fainting for His presence (Psa. 84:2). Our teams were thirsting for Him, and our flesh longing for Him, in a dry and thirsty land (Psa. 63:1). Our souls were panting for the living God, with tears as our food day and night. (Psa. 42:2) As it says in James 5:16, our prayers were effectual, and fervent and filled with unbelievable intensity, heat and passion for the unprecedented power of God to be made manifest for a people searching so earnestly for truth. We were being baptized with His desperation!

94

As the Holy Spirit usually awakens me with a verse or a word every morning, I get up and write. This time His words were etched deeply upon my heart. I picked up my pen and began to write.

"When penitent, persistent, pure-hearted, pleading and consistent prayer, together with a passionate pursuit for God's presence permeates His people, it will take priority and pre-eminence over plans, programs, performance, and people pleasing. It is then we will see His power poured out on the people across this planet."

Everything in our ministry was based on faith during this time. There was no set budget, no firm commitment of financial support from but a few people. Our monthly budget by now was around $50,000, yet we had no idea each month where this amount would come from, or if it would even come at all. Daily, I prayed to the Father, knowing He was the builder of His church, using our obedience to the voice of the Holy Spirit to accomplish His will. It reminded me of the little boy who shared his few fish and Jesus turned them into abundance. Daily I cried out to Him from my prayer closet,

"I have no Isaacs to lay on the altar, and no lunch to put in your hands, Father."

He gently reminded me to just be the lunch. And as I was put in His hands, day after day, He would tear me off, Jesus in me, and give me away, and there would always be enough with some left over.

After finishing a week of prayer and fasting with the team, I sat in my office and realized we had no money to continue. As I sat there reflecting on the widow who kept pouring out her oil, the Lord spoke to me gently, "Keep bringing in the vessels, the hurting and hungry hearts, and there will always be enough oil. Don't stop pouring, for the increase comes when you keep emptying out and giving away."

Suddenly the phone rang. I had never gotten a phone call from America, especially from someone I didn't know and who would know my number here.

"I am with a church in Oklahoma," a man's voice explained. "We have been given a large amount of money to give to a ministry in northern Uganda. When we went online, we found your website. The only criteria we have is that you have a ministry which lives the book of Acts."

"I assure you, we do," I answered and shared with him our stories.

Once again, the Lord had provided in a miraculous way, like He had done so many times before.

"To everything there is a season. A time to weep, and a time to laugh; a time to mourn, and a time to dance" Ecc. 3:1-4

What strong words Mordecai used with Esther. One day, they were spoken to us about our family in Uganda. "For if you remain completely silent at this time, relief and deliverance will arise for the Jews (Acholi) from another place, but you and your father's house will perish. Yet who knows whether you have come to the kingdom for such a time as this?" Esther 4:14

These were solemn words from the Lord and it was not long before we turned to Him with desperate prayer for a nation under attack. The US embassy emailed me with the news; Ebola had broken out in the last two weeks, spreading throughout the country faster than people had been aware. This deadly virus is passed on easily through skin moisture and bodily contact. This one had been moving quietly and quickly, stealing lives with a new strain, masking itself with malaria and flu-like symptoms. The fact it was Ebola had been undetected for almost three months and many had died by now, including some doctors in Kampala. We knew that if it reached a camp in northern Uganda, people could be dead in 2 weeks. The mortality rate was as high as 90%, with no treatment available. In addition to Ebola, cholera, hepatitis, and meningitis were also spreading in Uganda.

The WHO predicted, if it hit the camps, we could lose 45,000 people within three weeks.

The believers in the north rose up with an immediate and united cry for healing across the land. "If My people who are called by My name will humble themselves, and pray and seek My face, and turn from their wicked ways, then I will hear from heaven, and will forgive their sin and HEAL their land." (II Chron.7:14) That was the only answer any of us had.

The stadium field in Gulu was packed for overnight prayer on Friday night. The Mission House was filled for a week of prayer and fasting from Monday to Friday. An alert was being sent across the country by radio to churches, pastors, and believers... 'We MUST pray! We MUST seek His face and we MUST see God arise and his enemies scattered.'

"Arise, cry out in the night, at the beginning of the watches; pour out your heart like water before the face of the Lord. Lift your hands toward Him for the life of your young children." (Lamentations 2:19) This plea went out from every house and every heart throughout the land.

I was on the radio.

"Please, church, do not remain silent, at such a time as this! Stand with our brothers and sisters in the face of death, where physical contact as slight as a hand shake must be put on hold. In Acts 12, when the church prayed, prison doors were opened! Church, we MUST pray! God alone, not the government, and not medicine, can intervene in such a crisis fast enough to spare thousands of lives, which might otherwise be taken if these diseases sweep the nation without restraint.

David prayed for the plague in Israel to be stopped. After great repentance on his part, he stated, "...nor will I offer burnt offerings to the Lord my God with that which costs me nothing." The Lord heeded his prayers for the land, and the plague was withdrawn." (II Sam.24:24b,25b)

With my heart, full of faith and zeal, I told them, "God still has plans for this precious nation of Uganda. Believe with us for the fulfillment of Habakkuk 1:5, "Look among the nations and watch. Be utterly astounded! For I will work a work in your days which you would not believe, though it were told you."

God did hear, and He did answer. Because THE CHURCH prayed, God did what was impossible with man. It was phenomenal! Never had a plague been stopped in mid-stream before it took thousands of lives. The World Health Organization, Medical Reliefs and the Red Cross, UN or European Union could never have done what God did! Because we prayed, God Himself healed the land! (II Chron. 7:14).

On a Friday, I got a phone call from the hospital in Gulu, "Are you the people praying day and night?"

"Yes, we are," I answered, tired and weary by now.

"We want you to know, the five quarantined patients who have been held in isolation in the Gulu hospital, all tested negative and were sent home today. The plague has been stopped."

The Lord intervened, because many believers had pulled in from every corner of the field and got on their faces in united prayer. He reversed the curse once again. How great is our God!

Because of this miracle, He had taken our staff to another level by understanding faith is tested by fire to be refined as gold. It was at that point we learned to trust Him with impossible situations with the kind of faith which moves mountains, and encourage more water walkers to get out of the boat and see more nations delivered in a day!

In this faith, we could now pray Psalm 2:8 together, 'Ask of Me and I will give you the nations for your inheritance, and the ends of the earth for your possession.' We also prayed Isaiah 6:8, 'Whom shall I send, and who will go for Us?'

Once again, the cries of our team became, 'Here am I! Send me."

It was some time later, during another week on our knees, God tested us and proved His power in other impossible situations. The hospital had called Odong, one of our prayer leaders, asking him if they could bring some of the sick to our

House of Prayer. These were the terminally ill patients that were just 'waiting to die'. "We don't have enough beds for them."

"Yes, bring them over. If His house isn't a hospital for the sick, then I don't what it is," Odong answered without hesitation.

During the next few days, they didn't just bring one, but dozens of comatose and semi-conscious people, who were expected to be dead by morning.

When Odong informed me he had agreed to this arrangement, I said, "Good for you, Odong, we are truly the ER for this area, not just spiritually, but physically as well, it seems."

Our prayer teams sprang into action and walked from stretcher to stretcher as patients were laid out on the floor of our prayer house. The team began praying for miraculous healing for many days as one after another sick person rose from their cot. After they were up and healed, we kept them for another day to regain their strength and then released them to their families. The power of God fell in a mighty way as countless dying people miraculously recovered.

One man, comatose and in the end stages of HIV, was brought in, tied to several IV tubes. He was nothing but a pitiful skeleton on the verge of death. Our prayer team took turns praying for him, asking for the Lord to raise him up, because that was the only way he would see another day. Yet no matter how much we prayed, he did not improve. In spite of this, I declared, "God is faithful, He will raise him up."

His sister sat beside his cot, with a look of hopeless despair on her face.

"What happened to him?" I asked her.

"Two years ago, Odoch got involved in the occult and shortly after that, he became insane," she said. "He went mad, refused to eat and shriveled down to the skeleton you're looking at."

"Do you believe in the power of Jesus?" I asked her.

"I am Catholic, and yes, I do believe," she answered with hope in her voice.

The team continued to pray, but still, no response. Finally, I got so mad at the enemy holding him in bondage. I walked over to Odoch's cot and grabbed the comatose man by the arm, shouting with authority, "Satan, you are a liar and a thief and I am tired of you. I am here to kick you out in the Name of Jesus. I command you to leave this man and release him in the powerful, mighty Name of Jesus Christ!" I was still yelling when I turned to two of the team members, "Get him up and walk him around."

"But he is nearly dead and can't move," one of them said. "He is like a corpse already."

"Do it anyway. We're not believing with our eyes, but by faith, he will walk."

They pulled him up and held him under his arms, with his feet dragging behind him down the hall to the end of the house and back. They did that three times. By then he was using his feet and then walked on his own. Though he was still weak, he began to speak and then managed to take some soup. The next day, he was able to go home with his sister.

"Give him something good to eat to get his strength back." Before they left, I told her how to pray over him, and resist the devil. She prayed with us, in a fresh and renewed commitment to Jesus. I hugged them as they left the House of Prayer, never expecting to see them again.

Two years later, I was at a welcoming home party with sixty to seventy people there, when a young man walked up to me and said, "Do you remember me?"

I looked at him and shook my head. "I'm sorry, I don't."

"I'm Odoch, the man on the pallet whom you prayed for two years ago. Since then, the Lord healed me and helped me go back to school and get a diploma in communications and radio. I'm now working as one of your team. It was the occult that got me into the mess I was in and the Lord healed me and set me free."

Odoch grinned with the brightest smile and declared, "God gave me my life back and now I want to give it away."

In the midst of God performing mighty miracles with our teams reaching out 'into all the world', the enemy was busy as well. I felt a change in the atmosphere when I returned from a mission trip one day. It hung in the air like a dark cloud, a tension coming from internal strife among some of our team leaders.

I knew these staff members had been raised by fathers who had countless wives and sometimes dozens of children, whose names their fathers didn't even know. It had left them with a feeling of poor self-esteem, an orphan spirit and the constant need to grasp for something which wasn't theirs. I knew other ministries had dealt with this kind of problem, but this was the first time I sensed it in our own team. While God had done a deep work of healing their wounded spirits, and binding up the emotionally bruised, this was something different beginning to surface among the people working in the ministry.

I continued ministering, teaching and training as usual, and on the outside, all seemed normal. Until one day, I found out quite suddenly, that one of the leaders had been working for two years to take over the leadership position and was getting ready to dismiss me outright. While none of my staff had even known about this, he had gotten outside people to stand with him. Confused and broken-hearted, I turned to one of our board members, a father of fathers and a Godly man.

"I will quietly resign," I told him, "and let this man take over if that is what the Lord wants me to do. Maybe I can go to Sudan and start another ministry," I added, choking back the tears.

"You will do no such thing," he answered with confidence and strength in his voice. "You gave birth to this work, and you've carried the vision all these years. You are called to nurture it and will continue to lead."

I was amazed at the wisdom of this fatherly leader.

"Go on as usual, I will handle this." He sounded sure and it put my heart at peace.

Not long after, the rebellious leader packed his bags and, together with his co-conspirators, left. As I was praying about this I was reminded of Absalom, the son who betrayed King David. In spite of all he did, David continued to love him. Judas Iscariot also came to mind and I realized Jesus loved him to the very end and would have forgiven him if he had asked for it. I understood the Lord wanted me to do the same, and with much prayer I released to Him the pain I had felt at the betrayal. Would it always be a part of ministry, I wondered, and realized, Jesus was the only one I could ever truly trust.

Because of this, the year 2010 was a hard year and I learned many painful lessons. The saying is true that the darkness just before daylight is always the most difficult. The following year, 2011, proved to be a new and exciting advancement for the Kingdom of God, because once again, those of us on the team had gone through the fire.

Chapter 11

Follow in His Footprints

Since ancient times, the Sudan region has been an arena for interaction between the cultural traditions of Africa and those of the Mediterranean world. Islam and the Arabic language are spoken in many northern parts of the region, while older African languages and cultures predominate in the South. South Sudan won independence from the northern part of Sudan in a peaceful referendum in July 2011 after a sixty-two-year civil war.

As I was in prayer one day, I saw my tears falling on the feet of Jesus, loving Him so much, yet having so little to give. He leaned over and whispered to me, as I washed His feet with my tears, 'Now wash their feet, because as you do, you're washing mine. There must be many more following my footprints, climbing up lonely and rugged roads to get my message where it has never reached before. But only the feet of those willing to be truly 'pierced' will follow me if they are willing to die to themselves. Many will go back because the journey will be too hard or too long, but continue washing all the feet you can find and keep your eyes on mine, for where they step, you must also step, where they walk, you must also walk. Just as they were seen by my disciples just before I ascended to my Father, (Mark 16) and told them to 'Go, into all the world', so they will be seen again when I return and stand on the Mount of Olives (Zech.14). Follow after my footsteps and go to every tribe, every tongue and every nation I send you, for 'this gospel must be preached in all the world before the end will come' (Matt. 24:14). And I will make the place of my feet glorious (Isa. 60:13) if you put your feet in the footprints of mine!'

103

"But how will I know they are your footprints?" I asked, eager to understand what He was saying.

"I am following the voice of just one cry," Jesus answered tenderly, "leaving the 99 to go after just one."

"But I might lose sight of your steps, Lord," I persisted. "I must know I'm following your footprints and not another's."

"They will be the ones stained with blood." The tone of His voice was serious and I knew He was telling me to forsake all to follow Him.

I also realized the Lord was talking about South Sudan. Just as Uganda had been after the war, that land was crying out and desperate for Jesus. I knew He wanted us to reach out to this wounded, tortured country to the North, which had suffered from civil war for so many years, and take His message of salvation, love and forgiveness to its people.

While the harvest in South Sudan was ripe for the picking after the peaceful voting of the referendum for independence, there was still plenty of 'rumbling' between rural tribes over land, cattle, and age-old traditions. We continued to pray, the 'unsettling' within these remote tribal groups would make them more open to meeting the true Prince of Peace.

We had started to send teams in 2007 because even then I got many phone calls from pastors in Sudan. I'll never forget the first call for help. The man's voice was coming loud and clear through my cell phone from the top of a mango tree on top of a high mountain in Sudan. It was the only way he could get reception.

He sounded desperate, "Please, come, we've heard about the revival in Uganda. We need teaching and we need Bibles!"

Since I was too busy to go myself, I sent teams in 2007 with portable Bible schools and other evangelistic outreaches. It was not until the end of 2010, after the Lord spoke to me so clearly, I joined them. Our outreach to South Sudan started taking off after I sent Uganda missionary teams to go after the lost sheep of that nation. We began in earnest to equip Sudanese believers to become missionaries to their own people. To our surprise, we found many who were dissatisfied with 'a form of godliness that had denied a divine power to change them' through empty religious practices. Instead, they were desperate for an encounter with Someone alive and real! This desperation filled their hearts with the kind of spiritual hunger which helped them reject their former tribal beliefs and embrace the Gospel as soon as they heard it.

To help us in this outreach, the Lord made available to us a powerful missionary training curriculum called Orality Bible Story Telling. It was a wonderful resource for reaching not only non-literates, but ALL people with the treasures that lay buried in every single story in God's Word.

Teams from the US and Kenya began coming and helping us train the trainers, equipping almost 100 indigenous believers from Congo, Sudan and northern Uganda during our first conference. In time, by implementing this powerful way to teach, one after another of those who went out into the bush came back with the same testimonies, "What an amazing tool! It has helped us open their eyes and ours to the secrets within the scriptures like never before".

We began researching languages around Eastern Equatoria, a province of South Sudan, to see what Bibles there were available, if any, which needed to be translated into their languages, oral or written. Since 95% of rural Sudanese were non-literate, these orality tools became priceless instruments to plant the treasures of God's Word into hungry and searching hearts far more quickly than years of written Bible translations could have done. After the two-month Portable Bible schools, plus mission excursions every weekend into the mountain regions surrounding Torit, many souls were saved and several churches planted.

By God's grace, trained missionaries, pastors and church leaders continued to forge their way into these dangerous, mountain-dwelling tribes, which were buried deep in the bush and jungles of these mountainous regions around the Eastern edges of Southern Sudan.

Once again, God drew many men and women, refined by the fires of adversity, to help spread His Gospel with conviction and faith forged through personal experience.

One of those, a precious Sudanese pastor, Ohide, told us his story of fighting in the SPLM (Sudan People's Liberation Movement) for the freedom of his nation. When his troops were attacked by Arab gunmen, most of them fell dead. Realizing his only escape was to 'fall down dead' as well, he dropped among the bodies and covered himself with the blood of his fellow soldiers. As he listened to the Arabic speaking rebels talk of burying the bodies in a mass grave, he realized he would be buried alive unless he moved. Slowly, he crawled on his belly and elbows right through the midst of the Arab soldiers as God blinded their eyes. Undetected, he slid away into the jungle to freedom. He knew without a doubt his life had been spared by divine intervention because there was no way the enemy could have missed him as he crawled right past the rebels.

Shortly after his escape, he gave his heart to Jesus and promised to serve Him forever in the army of the Living God. When he came to us, he was eager for training and ready to reach the dangerous tribes for Jesus in the mountainous region around his home. In time, we worked with Ohide to help raise up, train and equip a whole 'army' of Sudanese soldiers. They were ready to saturate those remote areas with the love and power of the only true God by going into the hundreds of hidden villages deep in the bush.

My first trip to Torit, the largest town and the capital of Eastern Equatoria in South Sudan, proved to be a thirteen-hour, treacherous trek through isolated jungle terrain and endless swamps on barely visible dirt roads. I was accompanied by several of our team members and it was a miracle our car survived the journey through swamps, rough terrain and raging rivers. At one point, we were stuck in such deep, swampy mud, in spite of all our effort, we could not see any way to get the car out. It had sunk down so deep on one side, only one window was barely visible for us to crawl out to get to safety.

As the team and I sat on the side of the road praying for God to send help, we heard a group of people approaching. We had been warned of cannibalistic tribes and countless landmines in the area. The only way we had avoided the landmines, was looking for pink ribbons tied around trees to mark where they were buried.

How to avoid the cannibals was another matter. As we heard their voices getting closer, we had no way of knowing if we would end up as a meal for the tribe or be helped out of our dire situation. The only One who could protect us was the Lord. When a group of 'little men', they were of very small stature, reached us, their chatter increased when they saw our car stuck in the mud. Instead of harming us, they laughed while pointing at it and then left, leaving our group wondering what to do now.

Praise God, the little men returned with more men. Since it was obvious what was wrong, they began digging, laying rocks and other materials to steady the ground enough for the car to get traction. The entire time, they laughed and talked in an unknown language while throwing friendly glances at us every now and then.

Finally, after three hours, their leader motioned for me to start the car. Since the muffler was buried deep in mud, I had no idea what would happen, if anything. In the midst of flying mud and a lot of smoke shooting out from the muffler, our car slowly pulled out of the hole. A loud cheer went up among our good 'little' Samaritans.

Since I had nothing to give them in return for their help, I took out the Bibles I had brought and distributed them to each man. To my astonishment, they held them to their chest as if I had given them gold. I tried to tell them about Jesus in sign language, while pointing to the sky and the Bibles. They nodded their heads in joy and apparent understanding. I had no idea what they would do with books they couldn't read in a language they couldn't speak, but those Bibles seemed to mean everything to them. Maybe, in time the Lord would send someone to translate His Word for them.

Our vehicle sank into deep mud two more times during the remainder of our thirteen-hour journey. There was no way to drive around it, no way to escape it and no way to turn back. Finally, after crossing many checkpoints along the way, we arrived at the last one before Torit. The soldiers would not let us pass. They told us we had failed to get the right stamp on our passports from the jungle border patrol when we crossed the border. I was ready to cry as we sat there, covered with mud, unsure what to do. Instead of giving up, though, one of our team members spoke to the soldiers fearlessly, and with great spiritual authority he began preaching to them. When he came to the end of his simple salvation message, he asked them, "How many of you need to know this God, who created heaven and earth? Get down on your knees and accept Jesus into your heart."

Every one of them knelt down (!) and accepted the Lord and then waved us on. Praise God! When we arrived in Torit, still covered in mud and exhausted, the believers there were totally astounded we made the trip in spite of the dangers of the roads, the cannibals and the landmines. They were truly touched that we would have risked our lives for them attempting such a treacherous journey.

That night, I slipped into the little wooden bed feeling like I had just given birth to a nation. But that was only the beginning.

God proved true to His Word. South Sudan became a rich field, ripe for harvest as our teams were sent out to take the nation for the Kingdom. As a result of our November meetings in Torit, reports came in of hundreds saved, blind eyes were opened, crippled people walked. 'The book of Acts is repeating itself', the people marveled.

The first night of one of our open-air crusades in Torit, 30,000 people came. I had never seen so many people in one gathering! We had put on our posters that Jesus was in town, and would be doing the same things He did when He walked the earth in Bible days. People came from miles around, hungry and ready to be healed, saved and delivered.

The word of the mighty hand of God and His miracles spread across the land like wildfire. The next several nights, the crowds swelled to 50,000. The last night, the government officials who were there to control the crowds, counted 500,000.

Witchdoctors turned to salvation and burned their tools of witchcraft. Many people walked four or five hours and others traveled up to seven days from their villages and towns to attend the crusades. There was an intense hunger for the real power of God because people were fed up with the fear-induced demands of the powers of darkness which had ruled the region as well as the gods made of wood and stone.

God's power proved to be true and real, greater than any of the enemy's counterfeit. By the end of the week, thousands of people had turned to the Lord Jesus as their Savior!

As a result, the Governor of the State of Torit, in South Sudan, asked our team to go up into the mountain side, where the dangerous, naked villagers lived, accompanied by military escort. They were the main tribes responsible for the majority of the warring in this Eastern region. These aggressive villagers were greatly feared. Our team went willingly and preached the Gospel with such power that an entire village of 500 souls received salvation. God was on the ground and took back what the enemy had stolen! Word spread throughout the region, bringing deliverance from gripping fear, salvation and healing to the people of this land.

These crusades proved to be the 'tip of the spear' that pierced into the darkest of regions to 'break open' the atmosphere. They prepared the ground, which was the people's hearts, to receive the Word of God, which is the power of God! (Rom.1:16)

We stood amazed at how God began bringing about the re-birth of the nation of South Sudan. It all started when I had returned to America the last time and had stayed behind in the sanctuary of my church after a Wednesday night service, laying on the floor, praying, when I had a vision. In this vision, the Lord showed me pregnant and ready to give birth to a nation. I had no idea at that time He was talking about South Sudan.

God began bringing the reality of this to pass when I was in Kapeota, at the end of several large crusades which were attended by over 800,000 people from around the mountainous regions. In spite of these blessings, my heart still yearned to go where no one had wanted to go. I asked the Commissioner of the district to invite all the tribal chiefs from the villages and mountains around the regions of Kapeota, an area about three or four hours into the mountains. We sent messages by bicycle carriers and asked them to come for a dinner just outside of the house of the Commissioner.

A few days later, eighty of them came. We had bought a cow; the perfect way to honor them. Since there was a certain, ritualistic way to kill and eat it, so the chiefs could share in the dinner, we let them take care of the preparations. As everyone was seated on the bare ground, they brought in the entire carcass of the animal, cut up in large pieces, head and all, charcoaled and laying on a large wooden board.

The chiefs pulled leaves from the surrounding trees to serve as plates, sitting cross legged in small circles of about eight to a group. Each cut a large chunk of meat and passed it around to each of the chiefs, seated in careful, hierarchical order. While the meat looked perfectly black on the outside, the inside proved to be completely raw, with blood dripping to the ground as soon as they sliced it. From the looks of it, they thoroughly enjoyed the savory delicacy, and chatted amiably throughout the meal. When everyone had eaten their fill, they turned expectantly, ready to listen to me tell them about Jesus. When I finished my story about his saving love and death on the cross for each of them, every one of them raised their hands and bowed their heads to accept Jesus as their Savior. What a redemptive sight!

This dinner was the beginning of the government dinners we continued to hold everywhere we went from then on, bringing leaders of the nation together, feeding them a cow and seeing their hearts transformed through salvation. Our passion was to see them so changed, they would be ready to include Jesus into their culture.

As I sat with the eighty chiefs that evening, I wrote down the traditions which easily destroy a nation. I called them fruit killers, or better, root killers. As I wrote, I was reminded of the time the Lord gave me the vision on the church floor. These killers are cultural as well as demonic and have many names, such as corruption, polygamy, bloodshed, tribalism and witchcraft. They include inherited chore values like animal and human ritualistic killings, satanic worship, generational ideologies and anything which opposes the laws of the Kingdom of God.

These notes became the foundation of the teachings for the dinners we held from then on for commissioners, governors, mayors and military leaders across South Sudan. Exposing the root killers and destroying the fruit killers changed the hearts of the leaders and was the tool the Lord used to begin transforming this nation. It was truly amazing the favor we received from God and the leaders during this time of nation rebuilding.

These evangelistic, open-air meetings and government breakfasts were followed up by portable Bible School teams, ready to begin the two-month missionary and discipleship training program for the pastors and new believers. We always prayed for at least 200 to attend every one of these discipleship training schools so we could send them out as missionaries to their own language groups, reaching more of the hidden, unreached tribes surrounding Eastern Equatoria and every other region in which we held the outreaches.

One day, a lady from Juba, the capital city of South Sudan, called, "Please come up here. I have something for you."

When we arrived, there was excitement in her voice, "I heard how God turned the city of Torit upside down. Word of those meetings and what God did in transforming lives has reached me here in Juba. God touched my heart and told me to bless you. Come with me and pick out a brand-new land cruiser so God can use you to reach all the other places of South Sudan which are in desperate need of the Gospel of Jesus."

God had given us the wheels we needed to go where public vehicles could never go, helping us to equip His precious African Bride in having beautiful feet to take the Good News even farther!

We were excited about what was happening in the ministry. The Lord was moving in a mighty way across the countries of Uganda and now South Sudan. Uganda had seen a change in the very fabric of its foundation, starting with a change in people's hearts. We had seen God's hand on their land and heard His voice speaking revival, deliverance, healing and freshness throughout the regions.

The governments of South Sudan and Congo were so impressed with what God had accomplished through the vision and ministry of Favor of God, they began begging us to expand into their countries. They wanted us to bring education, medical help, trauma counseling, marriage & family counseling, Bible schools, discipleship training and children's homes to their nations.

Church plantings and construction programs were welcomed in every village. Out of these 'discipleship factories' grew prison outreaches, houses of prayer, youth and children's outreaches, education, crusades and evangelism. The churches became the hub and focal point of every village transformation and community development initiative.

They knew, with Bibles and resources brought in, village rebuilding would take place within their nation just as it had happened in Uganda. Due to the repeated requests by the South Sudanese governors and church leaders, Favor of God started conducting crusades across South Sudan, which again resulted in the blind seeing, the deaf hearing, the mute speaking, the crippled walking and the dead being raised! The harvest was ripe and the Lord had sent workers to bring it into the Kingdom!

In the meantime, at Gulu, it did not take long for our boys from House of Hope to move into our first finished building. These precious children continued to participate in various community outreaches, which they loved and begged to do. In the hospital, on the radio and through market evangelism, they were greatly used by the Lord in bringing healing and salvation to many.

The New Life Bible College building was finished and ready to house the Bible College. What an incredible leap forward in the continued equipping and preparation of African nationals to be 'sent out' as co-laborers into the Father's fields!

A grant came in for funding several Portable Bible schools throughout the next year in South Sudan and Uganda. Part of this money reactivated the extremely effective evangelistic Trauma Rehabilitation program, which was taken into these needy regions. A powerful dirt motorbike, which traveled well on the rugged dirt roads, was donated for the long distances of Portable Bible School mobilization and oversight.

We moved our Gulu clinic to a more economical rental site, more centrally located, in order to reach many more in the community of Gulu. Our primary school was now considered one of the highest quality schools, spiritually and academically. Friends gave generously for the excavation of a fish pond on our ten acres of land for the use and support of the children's village. This gave our children training in fish farming, as well as providing protein for the entire surrounding villages at the same time.

Our partnership with World Vision on their 'Rural Christian Leadership Program' started not long after. It was designed to bring Christian training to villages through the church, in families and the schools for the sake of developing a godly generation of children in the outlying village areas. They asked Favor of God to spearhead a portion of this vision as an international satellite project.

We ordered Bibles in many more languages and distributed them throughout the North as fast as the designated funding came through. In addition, we were increasing the orality resources and tools available for languages which had not yet been translated.

The House of Prayer for All Nations in downtown Gulu was filled to capacity daily for the noon-hour prayer gatherings. The community's hunger, unity and involvement for city-wide transformation continued to heighten as funds were given for the extension of the House of Prayer building, which was rapidly being outgrown.

God was moving in a mighty way in every direction we advanced in. Once again, I watched in awe as the power of God went before me as long as I followed in His footprints.

Chapter 12

Don't Call Me an Orphan

When you shape the life of a child, you are shaping the future of the world. What a responsibility and what a joy we had in training up the children who came to us at Favor Primary and the House of Hope Village. In our care, they continued to grow both in their testimonies and their commitment to the Lord. Their spiritual growth was a living reminder of God's miraculous power of redemption and the love our teachers and team leaders lavished on each of them.

Our House of Hope children learned the principles of leadership, academics, truth, trust and respect. New foundations, which had not been a part of their society in several generations before them, were laid in their lives. How it blessed us as we witnessed them celebrating their graduation from Primary to High School.

The enemy knows, to wipe out a civilization, he needs only to destroy its youth. The 20-year war of the Lord's Resistance Army targeted mainly the children of Uganda. They had faced continuous horror and death, forced to kill or be killed and watched friends and parents murdered before their eyes. Because of this, their normal childhood dreams were stolen or never had a chance to develop. We wondered, could these children, after such devastation, ever dream again?

What a reward it was to watch what happened when they were healed and made whole, overcoming their past and inspired and motivated to pursue a bright future. They learned to believe and trust again to achieve the goal to be what God had purposed for them to be, in spite of their violent past.

"Without a vision, my people perish" the Lord declares in His Word in Proverbs 29:19.

A good example of this is the story of a little girl named Lagum. She came to me one day with these words after she arrived at the House of Hope, "Look at my life. I have no parents, no family. What could I ever do, or what value would anyone see in me? I was born in poverty and have no future, I just exist."

After accepting Jesus as her Savior, we watched His truth fill her broken heart and answer the questions about who she was, why she was born and how much she was accepted by her Father and Creator. After she fully realized how much Jesus loved and believed in her, we saw Lagum's "grave clothes" begin to unwrap as she raised her face to look into the face of Jesus and found His love in the prayers and the faith of our Favor of God family, who surrounded and embraced her with unconditional love and care.

A large part of our ministry was to help free these children and bind up their shattered hearts after having been born into brokenness, rejection, sin, despair and disappointment, and begin exposing them to the love of Jesus and the love of our staff at the House of Hope.

I realized, without a doubt, the children in the west were no more valuable to the Lord than these just because they were born into a stable environment and with their families intact.

To me, these precious African children were every bit as priceless and, therefore, should have the same opportunity to dream, hope and grow up into a bright, successful future.

One day, Lagum asked me, "Can I really be a doctor some day? Do you think I can, Mum?"

"Yes, Lagum, you can live the very dreams and desires God puts in your heart. You can, Lagum, you can!" I added with great conviction.

"Who will go with me, Mum?" she asked, her eyes fastened on me. "I may get tired along the way, lose hope, or have no money to finish my schooling. Who will help me?"

"God is there, Lagum, and He always will be, even when I'm not. He's your Father who will never leave you, the provider who will not forsake you, the comforter who will always hold you and His strength will always inspire you, even if everyone else fails."

"I know He is, Mum, I really believe that. But, oh, how I would love to see Him, especially when I need His help so much."

"You have seen Him, Lagum, because you see Him in us. We will run with you, help you when you fall and encourage you when you are down." I hugged her. "We will be there for you and will see you through until you reach your dreams."

As I said those words, I knew the Lord had ordained me to be part of the body of Christ, walking with His feet, reaching out with His loving arms and guiding me through His Holy Spirit. All of us at the House of Hope were willing to run the race with each of these little ones, as their faith soared, their lives changed and they could believe God for their purpose and in turn change their people and their nation.

Lagum, as young as she was, developed into quite a mighty prayer warrior.

"When can I go preach, Mum?" she would beg each time I got ready to go to South Sudan. She and her brother Ogen, who also stayed with us, were part of a team of prayer warriors which moved heaven and made angels stand at attention. With the rest of the children, they could not wait to come in from play each day to worship with the odongo, an African musical instrument. There would be dancing, singing and shouting to the Lord, combined with passionate prayer and intercession. This group of children would fall before the Lord and petition Him with great faith and passion. There was no way I would have ever left on a mission trip without asking these 'victims turned warriors' to intercede for me with the Father because the Lord had taken broken pieces of clay and turned them into beautiful vessels of His power in the Kingdom.

Prayer that moves heaven and makes angels stand at attention

A few years later, we rejoiced with Lagum when she was called into the government office here in Gulu to receive honors amongst her peers for excellence in academics and leadership. She had graduated highest among the girls in the district.

Over the years, she was just one of many we have loved, nurtured and trained to walk into destinies of godly lives and leadership. We watched many of these youths as they went back into their villages, communities, families and schools, reaching out with great understanding and compassion because they remembered where they, too, had come from.

How awesome it was to know the Lord used us at the House of Hope to set a new generation free to be the dreamers God created. How blessed we were to have walked with them through mountains and valleys, victories and defeat, until they became the leaders they were called to be. We were witnesses of how one decision could change a destination and one life could change a nation.

In time, most of these children were resettled in their birth village. The Ugandan government encouraged all long-term children's homes to do this so these orphans could grow up with a loving, natural relative. Their plan was to allow them to be with us for three to five years and then resettle them in their original birth clan. They still remained "our" children physically and spiritually as we continued to supervise, educate, train, nurture and love each of them on a regular basis. Our loving social worker team from the House of Hope kept in close touch with them, visiting and overseeing their medical care, spiritual development and education.

The transformation of some of these children from traumatized, starving orphans into powerful leaders in the Kingdom was incredible to watch.

Another example of this was a boy, eleven years old, named Okot. Like all the others, he was a total orphan after losing his parents in the war. He was a quiet child, or so I thought, until one day, during a conference we held at the House of Hope, he asked if he could give his testimony. To my astonishment, he took the microphone and turned into a fiery preacher with these words, "Don't you ever call me an orphan! I have a Father who adopted me and who loves me more than my earthly father ever could." He went on to preach salvation and how to walk with the Lord in righteousness and power.

As I listened, it confirmed to me once again, we had done more than give physical and mental help to him and the other children in our home. We had also been God's instruments of setting them free from the strong spiritual bondage of the occult. Okot and the other children learned scriptural principles and how to walk in the power of God through prayer, deliverance, perseverance and trust in the Lord.

They knew how to take back the territory the enemy had stolen by coming against the forces of darkness, so prevalent in their nation. Without teaching them this most important aspect of Christianity, we would simply have been putting band-aids on demons, because without it, all the schools, all the human programs and religious teachings would have had little effect on their long-term walk with the Lord. Without the interference of the enemy, they were then able to learn to trust God and His power, instead of their own.

As for Okot, he has become a powerful worship leader, intercessor and dynamic preacher. His goal is to become a doctor, and I have no doubt, the Lord will be right there to bring it about. As to the other children, just like him, they are "going out into all the world" as they witness, preach and prophesy, declaring the miracles of God on radio once a week, as well as in the hospital and in their churches. Still teenagers, they have truly become leaders and are tools to bring revival to their villages and nation.

Jesus' church is made up of living stones with precious people as building blocks whom He died to redeem. Just like these children, it is His heart which says 'none should perish, but that all should come to repentance.' (II Peter 3:9). His church, here and across the world, is made up of those who once were outcasts. He came for the lame, the blind and bleeding and died for the rejected, the wounded and broken-hearted, the imprisoned, crippled, forgotten, maimed and hungry. And not just here, but wherever we happen to live. He has given us all a purpose to reach out to them, wherever we may live, whether in Africa or in our neighborhoods.

When we find these, we find God. (Matt. 25:45)
When we love these, we love God. (John 14:21)
When we serve these, we serve God. (John 13:12-17)

When we have laid our lives down for these, we have laid our lives down for God. (John 15:12, 13)

When we haven't found these, we haven't found God.

When we haven't served these, we haven't served God.

When we haven't loved these, we haven't loved God.

When we haven't laid our lives down for these, we haven't laid our lives down for God.

And whether we live in Africa or America, whether in the Middle East, across the world or in our own neighborhood, our mission field is right there. It may not look like it, but our neighbors in Michigan, California or anywhere else in "our world", are the hurting people, those longing for a purpose in the midst of an evil, confusing world, searching for answers. WE HAVE IT! Let us give to them the greatest gift we could ever give in the form of the love of Jesus and His Gospel, wrapped in the Word of God, called the Bible, and the word of our testimony.

It is impossible to love God unless you love your neighbor as yourself. Whether your friends and neighbors live in Africa or in the house next door, if you don't share salvation with them or reach out with His love, they will be cut off from an eternity with Jesus. If you are embarrassed or afraid to give freely what you have freely received, start trusting in the Lord like the children in Africa, who dare to expect the power of God to do what they cannot do. Remember, you cannot convince anyone of their need for salvation, only the Holy Spirit can. All you have to do is to be willing to serve as the messenger of His Word; He will do the rest.

As you read about the mighty wonders and miracles in this book, dare to be jealous and ask God right now to do in your life what He is doing in a far-away land called Uganda. Like a child, go to Him and give Him your life in order to be used by Him for His Kingdom and then watch in awe at what He might do through you.

If you have never given Him your life, allow me to pray for you right now this simple prayer of faith:

Heavenly Father,

I come to you with the faith of a child. I am a sinner and I am sorry for my sins. My life is broken and my heart longs for your forgiveness. I give it to you just as it is and ask you to heal it, mend it and renew it just like you do with those children in Africa. Take my life as you took theirs and use me in your Kingdom and for your Glory. I don't know how to do anything on my own, but through your Son, Jesus Christ, I can do all things. Thank you for sending Him to die for me. It is hard to believe you love me that much, but your Word says you do, and I believe you. In Jesus Name. Amen.

Playing the traditional African Harp

A witchdoctor before meeting Jesus

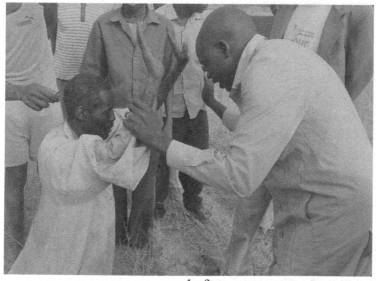

…and after

Chapter 13

From Satan's Agent to God's Ambassador

As we all know, God never gets tired, but neither does the enemy. We found ourselves in a place of being overwhelmed, but in a good way, as the Lord was impressing on me in prayer,

'Ask me for the nations.'

I knew this could only be done through intensive prayer and spiritual warfare. We seemed to be in a fight of survival in an unusual sort of way. I felt I needed an army to keep pressing in, because the enemy was pulling out all the stops to keep us from going forward through spiritual warfare in the form of internal strife, take-overs and other hindrances against the ministry.

Prayer became my manna and hiding place. While talking to the Lord one day, I was reminded of a time before I came to Uganda several years ago, when I was asked to meet with an African Bishop. Although I didn't know why I should, I agreed. He turned out to be a white man in his sixties, a wise and seasoned servant of God.

"I hear you are going to Northern Uganda where the war is," he said as we sat down to talk. "God help you. I have worked for years in Ghana and know well the demonic forces operating in those countries within every aspect of society. They will not leave just because you hold a large crusade, for they understand the history and pattern. That without follow-up, usually nine out of ten of those who accept Jesus, will return to their old state and the practice of the occult. Therefore, the enemy won't bother with you much if that is your plan. However, if you equip the local church and disciple their leaders with a vision of bringing lasting transformation in the land, the devil will come against you with all the forces of hell he can muster. That will include violence and human sacrifices if necessary. The only way to combat him is by getting a solid prayer covering in America as well as in the area you are going."

As I reminisced about our conversation, I realized I was living in the midst of the fury of Satan, because we were going into South Sudan, not just for a crusade, but to equip the saints and 'take the land'. It was as if I was swimming against a mighty stream and would drown in despair if I did not become desperate for God in the midst of overwhelming obstacles. I needed a group of warriors on fire; men and women turned on by intense prayer to bring down the Glory and victory in South Sudan. It would be an uphill battle because these people had not just had twenty years of civil war, but over sixty! During that time, the enemy had plenty of time to become entrenched in their minds and hearts with an iron grip of unimaginable strength and intensity.

At the House of Prayer, we felt surrounded by the forces of Satan, especially in the area of our prayer life. I knew, without it, we would be powerless victims of confusion, take-overs and any other onslaught of hindrances in this fierce battle of spiritual dominance. In holy desperation, we turned to God for help as we engaged in a desperate effort of continuous prayer on a daily basis. I knew nothing else would or could help us press forward in our quest to conquer "the nations" like God had impressed upon me to do.

It was a regular morning. After I had returned to Gulu from an extended trip the day before, a young Acholi man walked into my office.

"Mum, can I talk to you?" He looked around nervously as I motioned for him to sit down in front of my desk. He fidgeted with his hands and then took a deep breath, "My name is Okelo and I need to tell you the truth. I understand you can get me arrested and have me put away for life for what I have done, but the Lord tells me to talk to you."

"Okelo, don't worry, you are a new creation in Christ Jesus. Tell me what is on your mind," I said with a reassuring smile.

125

He took a deep breath before he went on.

"I am the nephew of Joseph Kony from Odek village."

Now it was my turn to take a deep breath.

"Go on, I'm listening."

"When I was twelve years old, a friend introduced me to the occult, deep in the bush, where these servants of Satan meet. They were not ordinary witch doctors, but agents of Satan and agents of Kony with deep connections to the underworld. One even claimed to be the right-hand agent to Lucifer himself. He told me he had a right to me since I had been dedicated to him at birth.

In time, I became totally immersed in the kingdom of Satan and, the longer I was involved, the more I experienced his immense power. One way to increase it in me was by killing as many people as possible. At first, it was suggested I participate in this, but soon, I had no other option but to kill a certain number or be killed. I answered to Akim, who was third in command to Kony, and my superior." Okelo looked at me with a strange, apprehensive expression on his face, waiting for me to allow him to go on.

I nodded.

"Five years ago, I was assigned by Akim to take you out or I would be killed." He leaned forward, "Do you remember all the robberies during those years that you thought were committed by the violent youth in Gulu, who had been LRA rebels? I must tell you, I was their leader. There were many times I entered your house with my fellow gang members, armed and determined to kill you. When I couldn't, I would help steal things like your computer and whatever else was in reach."

"Why couldn't you go through with it?" I asked, astonished, because I remembered during that time, I hired more and more guards to protect the house but nothing prevented the break-ins.

"I tried, I really did, but you were covered with the blood of Jesus. It was like a shield I couldn't penetrate; a wall of fire which was impossible for me to break through."

126

I leaned back and remembered a time of prayer I had with the Lord when I first came to Uganda.

"I have no plan, no money, no assignment, no organization or instructions, Lord. Please, give me one verse and one assignment that will carry me in this nation." He led me to the book of Haggai, which talks about rebuilding the House of the Lord which lay in ruins. And then He led me to Mark 11:17 which says, "My house shall be called a House of Prayer for all nations." That was my assignment from Him.

But the verse I have lived by all these years was the promise He gave me at that time, found in Zechariah 2:5, 'And I will be a wall of fire around about you, declares the Lord, and I will be the Glory of God in the midst of you.'

As Okelo spoke, I was overcome with wonder because I heard the same thing coming from his mouth.

"As hard as I tried, my finger was not allowed to pull the trigger to kill you, nor was I able to lay a hand on the House of Prayer team," he went on. "The longer it went on, the bigger the threats I received from Akim. He wanted me to destroy all the houses of prayer because he knew those were the places where the power came from which was stripping from him his own powers of darkness. I couldn't touch you, Mum, no matter how hard I tried."

He looked at me with a look of shame and continued, "I remember the night I was in your room and watched as you came against the forces of evil, when suddenly a snake came at you and you wrestled with it. Since you were protected by the blood as if you wore a shield, I knew God was on your side and there was nothing I could do. In defeat, I left without letting you know I had been there."

I realized, the Lord had kept His promise to protect me from all evil just as He said He would. I had a hard time continuing to listen to Okelo's story as he went on, "During this time, I took a wife and she had a baby. She was a Christian and prayed for me daily at the House of Prayer. She challenged me to accept the Lord but it only made me go further into the occult. I advanced rapidly in the ranks as I walked deeper and deeper into the darkness, until I was put in charge of several witch doctors.

To prove myself to Akim, I was commanded to bring fifty souls as a sacrifice every so often. If I didn't, they would kill my baby."

"How did you manage to kill fifty people at a time without getting caught?" I asked with astonishment.

"That was easy," he answered in a monotone voice, "There are several intersections in Gulu. A group of us would conjure up chaos and it would result in an accident with several fatalities at a time. If I failed to do what I was asked, my little girl would suddenly develop severe breathing problems and nearly choke to death each time I disobeyed the occult leader. I would beg Akim to give me another chance and not kill her. The next day I would go out and cause another accident, and again, causing many to die.

My wife would not give up on me and continued to challenge me to try Jesus and be free from my bondage. I got very angry one day and went to the House of Prayer to bring chaos and destruction and find her and drag her out. One of your team members was sharing the Gospel and then taught on the blood of Jesus. At the end, he gave a word from the Lord, "There is an agent of the devil in the room and he has come here to bring death and destruction. God has brought you here to set you free."

"When I heard this, I fell to the floor, writhing and foaming at the mouth in a grand mal seizure. It lasted for quite a while, until, exhausted, I sat up and gave my life to Jesus."

"I remember," I said with a smile.

Okelo stayed at the House of Prayer for a year, learning, praying, and growing in the Lord. At one time, he asked us to go with him to pray at the intersections in Gulu town, which used to be his "post of duty" and the site of the horrific bloodshed he caused. At 5 a.m. one morning, we knelt in the dirt and came against the evil, demonic forces which had caused the chaos and horror. Ever since then, no more accidents have occurred in that area.

Okelo began to witness in door to door evangelism and lead entire families to the Lord with his powerful testimony. Signs, wonders and miracles followed him wherever he went. Since then he has been called specifically to witness to the Muslims, winning many to salvation.

He has become one of our greatest intercessors and to this day, when I need help with a demonic attack I cannot overcome alone, I call on him. He immediately comes against the dark forces so familiar to him from his past in a most powerful way; overcoming their powers by applying the Name of Jesus and His blood during a time of intense intercessory prayer. It is remarkable, the very agent Satan sent to destroy me, is now used by God to deliver me.

Prayer makes the difference between life or death and is not an option for any Christian. Because many of you have prayed, there can be no doubt, while God sent me here, your prayers have kept me alive.

Chapter 14

Elephants or Termites

South Sudan is the only Arabic speaking nation in Africa which is not Muslim-ruled. It is one of the richest nations when it comes to natural resources and, therefore, a target for many surrounding countries to take it by force. For over sixty years, it has been steeped in internal strife and civil war which has left it devastated and wracked in poverty, violence and the occult.

And yet, this was the place God had chosen for me to go next. I knew I was destined to become a part in preparing its people for "such a time as this" to arise and take the Gospel northward, into the Muslim and Arabic speaking nations. I had a strong feeling. This was "the proper time" to take the power of the Gospel through radical prayer and preaching, followed by signs, wonders and miracles to reach these nations which were previously closed to the Word of God. What a destiny! Zephaniah 3:9-10 was one of the prophetic passages spoken to me which says, 'Then I will purify the lips of the peoples, that all of them may call on the name of the Lord and serve him shoulder to shoulder. From beyond the rivers of Cush, my worshipers, my scattered people, will bring me offerings.'

The Cushite people are mentioned over 140 times in the Bible with promises of blessing, favor, abundance and God's high calling on their lives as a nation. We were praying in the land of the Cushites, which should have been their new name as a nation when it got its independence. Though the western nations refused them that title, God did not refuse them. His promises are "yes" and" amen", and they still stand strong for a nation He has called and ordained to take His Word to the ends of the African continent; right into Muslim territory!

130

Many times, the Lord seemed to use one person in particular before we start to reach out to a new group of people. It was the same in South Sudan when we began with our witness to the Muslims.

His name was Ahmed. He was a successful and staunch Muslim with the rank of major in the South Sudanese army. He came to Uganda in search of his parents who had fled the war. After he had exhausted all his resources in the hunt, he discovered they had passed away. Destitute and in despair, Ahmed began the 170 miles walk back to South Sudan, contemplating suicide on the way because after a life of faithful commitment to Islam, Muhammad or Allah had not, or could not, help him.

As he walked through Gulu, Ahmed passed by our House of Prayer and heard singing. In desperation he thought, *'I have tried everything else. Before I end my life, I will try Jesus.'* When he entered our prayer gathering, ragged, thin and bedraggled, wearing his Muslim hat, he knew exactly 'what', or better, 'who' he was looking for. He had come to find Jesus! Without hesitation, he walked down to the front and got on his knees, weeping and sobbing like a baby as he cried out, "Can He really love me? Can He really forgive me?"

We stopped our worship, gathered around him and prayed with him to receive Jesus, as our young men in leadership knelt in front of him and embraced him like a long-lost son.

Instantly, the presence of God was immensely powerful and the scene was like something right out of heaven as this prodigal son discovered the love of his heavenly Father. As we stood around him, we wept with him and showered him with the love of the body of Christ, leading him into his Damascus road experience.

"May I tell my story?" Ahmed asked, after he wiped his face and stopped his tears.

"Please do," I said eagerly.

"I was born a Muslim and raised to believe in the Koran all my life. I learned killing in the army and saw worse atrocities than you could ever imagine. I experienced so much bloodshed and killed so many people in battle, it affected my mind. I couldn't sleep at night and when I prayed to Mohammed to help me, he couldn't. I had horrible dreams about blood and would go into the graveyards at night looking for someone to kill. When I couldn't find any blood to shed, I started cutting myself and then sucked my own blood, overcome by bloodthirstiness. I couldn't stop and knew I was going mad. No one could help me. I came here, ready to take my life when I found out my parents were dead. What else did I have to live for? That's when I remembered, I had heard about this prophet Jesus, who could give life, and came back from the dead. I decided, as a last resort, I would give Him a try before I took my life. But I didn't know where to find Him. I have wandered for days, with no food, until I heard the singing from this house and I came in. And this is where I found Him."

What joy and celebration broke out in the House of Prayer that day. We had been on our faces, weeping for the nation of South Sudan and its Muslims to come to Jesus, when this South Sudanese Muslim walked in and gave his heart to Jesus.

Afterwards, we gave him a Bible and he joined us in worship for the rest of the day. That night, our young men invited him to eat with them and to stay in a room at the House of Prayer. One of our staff remained with him and they read the word together into the evening.

When I saw Ahmed the next morning, he was clean and dressed in the clothes our team had given him.

He smiled and said, "I ate pork last night for the first time. It was really good!" The team laughed.

Ahmed's face was radiant, as if he had just seen heaven. Over breakfast he told us, "This is the dream Jesus gave me in the night when He spoke into my heart." He cited the names of three cities in South Sudan and said, "Jesus told me to go to these cities and talk about His salvation to whomever I meet. Even if it's under mango trees, I will preach about Him wherever He may lead me. But first I have to go back and tell my family that both my parents are dead. Then I will tell them about the decision I have made to follow Jesus. I am a Christian now. I know I will face persecution but I will preach about Jesus the rest of my life. Even though they may kill me, I would rather die for the truth from now on, than live for a lie."

Ahmed completed our Bible school and trauma counseling programs after he returned. He read through the entire Bible and then started preaching in the prisons, at open air crusades, in villages and churches with our ministry teams. Although he was rejected by his remaining family when they learned of his conversion, his passion for Jesus never wavered. As fast as he learned about his new faith, he taught others. It was his greatest desire to become a missionary to Khartoum in Sudan. God used him in a mighty way to reach those of his former faith to tell them of the changing power of the real God – Jesus Christ. Ahmed's life encapsulates our whole vision for South Sudan at Favor of God and demonstrates the powerful impact it has on the lives of individuals and entire communities! He is just one of the many we were privileged to stand alongside, as each day, they walked through the process of transformation. We continuously pray for the Muslims to embrace the true God and turn from hatred and violence toward their enemies, to love them like Jesus commands. It is the only way to turn the tide of Satan's curse all over the world and defeat terrorism.

Soon enough we became aware of the purpose for which the Lord had raised Ahmed up. South Sudan was fighting against the onslaught of Islamic regime and domination from North Sudan. South Sudan was the gateway of their Muslim faith, from northern Africa, into the South and the rest of the African countries. Since the national language of South Sudan is Arabic, this nation would be the perfect tool for the Lord to use in reaching the Muslim world in the northern countries of Africa, to bring them to Jesus.

South Sudan is a land with a rich history. It is vast and mysterious, containing among other wonders, pyramids like those in Egypt. Within its massive tracts of unexplored swampland, lay rich oil fields, gold and other precious metals. Yet, it is its people who are one of its richest treasures.

The South Sudanese people have been pharaohs, like King Tirhakah, the Cushite (Sudanese) Pharaoh, whose advancing army drew Sennacherib away from the besieged Hezekiah in Jerusalem (2 Kings 19:9). At the same time, they have also been slaves, like Ebed-Mekel, the Sudanese eunuch who rescued Jeremiah from slow starvation in a well (Jer. 38).

Their pharaonic Kingdom spanned from the land of Cush to the Mediterranean Sea. Yet their history of enslavement is a much less glorious story. While Christianity came to Cush through Philip's encounter with the eunuch of Queen Candace's court and ruled as the governing religion from 543-1315AD, slavery continued to plague the nation. They were the required tribute to keep the powerful Muslim neighbors to the north at bay. In the end, this arrangement failed and even today, thousands are abducted from South Sudan and sold as slaves in Khartoum and northern African nations.

This history of South Sudanese bondage is not purely physical. It is also deeply spiritual. Bonds of violence, bloodshed, witchcraft and Islam have kept the people in years of darkness and bondage in spite of the successful vote for freedom in 2011.

It was at this time, God was doing a new thing among the people of South Sudan. In Isaiah 18, we see His word concerning the Cushite people: 'Woe to the land of whirring wings along the rivers of Cush, which sends envoys by sea in papyrus boats over the water. Go, swift messengers, to a people tall and smooth-skinned, to a people feared far and wide, an aggressive nation of strange speech, whose land is divided by rivers. All you people of the world, you who live on the earth, when a banner is raised on the mountains, you will see it, and when a trumpet sounds, you will hear it. At that time, gifts will be brought to the Lord Almighty from a people tall and smooth-skinned, from a people feared far and wide, an aggressive nation of strange speech, whose land is divided by rivers. The gifts will be brought to Mount Zion, the place of the Name of the Lord Almighty.'

The prophet Isaiah speaks of sadness and destruction, which has been experienced deeply, but he also speaks of the return of the Lord's favor as indicated by Him, turning His face to "look on" the Cushites once more as they bring their gifts to Him, the Lord Almighty.

In 2013, there was a big Islamic push into South Sudan, not with an army, but from the inside. Two tribal leaders, one of them who had been allied with Muslim leaders, were pitted against one another, which caused constant division, retaliation and internal conflict in every area of the government. Added to that, China entered the fray because South Sudan is rich in oil. To make things worse, as in Uganda, every area of life was still very much influenced by the occult and the countless, evil practices that come with it.

There was no doubt, no human weapon formed against these forces could even begin to prosper unless the Lord intervened. By the year 2015, I realized it would have to be a spiritual awakening, brought about by the spiritual power of the living God, if we were to spread the Gospel in the midst of this broiling caldron of hatred, violence and war between the different forces of evil in that nation.

The believers in and around Juba were losing hope as the fighting increased. They had endured over sixty years of war already, which now continued in spite of the referendum of 2011, and they were tired of fighting.

In 2013, I began organizing a successful pastors' and leaders' conference in order to encourage believers and church leaders to rise up and never give up. Over 300 attended, and the

135

meetings were successful and refreshing, as a visiting team from the US came in for the teaching and medical outreaches.

As the conference came to a close, I met with a group of pastors from the area of Juba. We sat on the ground in a big circle under a large, shady tree. For some reason, I sensed a mood of discouragement and sadness as I addressed them.

"The Spirit of God is here. It will remain if you walk out the victory and take the land and occupy it," I said.

"There is no way we can do that." They spoke in a low, discouraged tone. "We don't have anything. No money for building churches or the speakers and sound systems needed to preach the Gospel. We have no vehicles and all the other things needed to bring the people in."

After listening, I told them that I was reminded of a story a missionary told in a book about the underground church in China. It was when communism took over and the believers were put in prison for their faith. Missionaries evacuated and the Christians were left to fend for themselves. And yet, amazingly, the church exploded!

"Let me tell you the reason why," I went on. "When an elephant comes into a village, the earth shakes as the elephant crushes everything in its path and knocks over trees, making loud noises as it eats and stomps through the bush. But then it is gone and very little has changed in the village, except some smashed grass and broken tree limbs.

This conference was like that elephant. What we saw was powerful and shook the earth, but it will not change anything in the long run. Now it's up to you."

They looked at me, nodding their heads in understanding as I continued, "The termites are different. They come from all directions, underground and unnoticed by anyone. They come in large numbers and quietly go to work, eating the foundation of a house until the building collapses and then go on to the next. No one knows they are there."

I leaned forward and smiled. "You are God's army of termites. If you are willing to remain faceless, dead to self and underground, you will destroy the foundation of the culture of evil in this land until it crumbles and no one will even know you did it. You may not get any glory and no one may ever know about you but the power of God will accomplish, through your hidden and united efforts, what we could never get done alone, in one great big event."

Their faces were shining by now as they broke out in radiant smiles.

"Mum, we can do it! It doesn't take any money and yet we will bring in a harvest of souls, just as you've said, and bring down the forces of evil, just like we've watched you do through prayer."

I realized then we had left the Word of God in good hands.

By 2015 God began to stir my heart to see a new foundation in South Sudan, restored and rebuilt. I truly felt it was God's plan; that the country must fulfill its divine destiny so the Lord might use it to plunder the gates of hell and increase heaven, until all men might hear the Gospel. God is the only way and the only One who could reconcile the tribes, bring healing to the government and society and achieve the transformation of this land into His Sudanese Bride. While this seemed an impossible goal, our God is the God of the impossible!

Chapter 15

How do You Measure God's Glory?

This word was beginning to be fulfilled as gifts of prayer, repentance and worship were raised to the Lord during the National Prayer Gathering in the stadium in Juba in July, 2015.

It all started with me driving to South Sudan by myself because I strongly felt the anointing of the Lord to go there. The reason I went alone was that there was a $50 visa fee for each person to cross the border into South Sudan and I did not think I could afford to take any of our team members.

When I got there, Mudasia, a good friend and prayer warrior from Kenya, met me in Juba. We were joined by one other pastor who agreed to pray and help me organize the National Prayer Gathering in the city.

South Sudan was just as North Uganda had been, filled with occult practices and tribal rituals, witchcraft and generational curses and locked in turmoil, bloodshed and upheaval. I knew, just as He had done there, God would have to overcome these with His power through the fervent, passionate and continued prayer of committed believers.

"We don't need a committee," I told them when I got there. "And neither do we need to consult any man." (Galatians 1:16)

The pastor I found was Musa, a Bible student from my first days of teaching in the Bible school in Kampala. He had since become a missionary in the area and agreed to help. Together with Musa and Mudasia, we set out to do as the Lord had shown me.

"The first thing we do is call for a forty-day fast. Musa, try to get forty churches to participate, each one taking one full day of prayer and fasting. Then sign up twenty-four people in each church to agree to cover one of the one-hour prayer slots in that day until you have every slot filled for every day, one church at a time," I began.

"Mudasia, you concentrate on the hosting and find enough people to help you. I also want you to make a longer prayer guide for South Sudan and its Cushite history that people can take home and pray over. Musa, we will need to announce it on radio, TV, newspapers and distribute thousands of flyers as well as posters and banners to reach every person in Juba. I will put together a prayer guide for the week we will be meeting in the stadium for prayer, using the verses on repentance, revival and restoration that God has put on my heart."

Since we had no money, the matter of renting the large culture center in Juba loomed large in my mind. Also, the director turned out to be a Muslim. When I could postpone it no longer, I went to him and said, "It is time for you to bow your knees to Jesus. We are coming to pray against your god."

"I don't care who you pray to," he said with a smile, "as long as you pay the $20,000 it costs to rent the center for a week."

"I will take it and you will get your money by the end of the week." I didn't tell him I didn't have a dime. Not one. I got on my knees and pleaded with the Lord, "God, show your name in a strong way and supply the money." Then I picked up the phone and called a dear friend in America. I said to her, "I need a miracle by the end of the week. Can you help?" I pleaded.

"How much money do you need?" she asked. I told her. "I will send it tomorrow," she said without hesitation.

Hundreds began to come. As praises rose each day, we witnessed chains begin to break off of those who gathered. The event itself was a miracle as we saw government leaders welcome the idea with passion and agree, this was God at work! They said, "This has never been done in this nation and it has brought a new unity among churches."

For the first time, all church denominations and many political leaders gathered together in one place with one objective: to seek God's hand for repentance, revival and restoration in their land. And as the people prayed and praised – God answered with amazing miracles, "turning things upside down." People were saved, healed and delivered from darkness into the light and hope of the Gospel!

We sang the Word and prayed it, worshiped at the altar of the Living God, Jesus Christ. We gathered around His throne with one voice, one heart, one tribe and one nation, though many. Jesus, the spotless Lamb, was lifted up every day over this land. His blood was poured out over South Sudan, to cover the blood of thousands of murdered men, women and children, and wash this nation clean as fresh fallen snow. We prayed for eleven hours a day, for seven days, and over 1,000 people gathered at different times.

God had put the prayer strategy upon my heart and the scripture verses were written and prayed over, read by South Sudanese, leading the group.

There were two days of scriptures dealing with repentance for eleven hours. A Sudanese leader, from the government, church, business or intercessor would read the scripture and lead the throngs of people in prayer over their nation, according to that passage.

Then, two days of scriptures concerning revival, covering eleven hours each day. After that, two days of reading scripture and prayer regarding restoration in the land, for eleven hours. Lastly, a day of God's word in praise and thanksgiving for eleven hours.

There were altogether seventy-seven hours of prayer which covered the stadium and filled the heavens, as Jesus our Great High Priest prayed with us over the healing of this land.

There were Sudanese exiles from the north, as well as refugees, who had fled for safety to Juba from the northern states of Jongeli, Unity, Upper Nile and other places of intense bloodshed and fighting. There were Ethiopians, Kenyans, Ugandans, Botswanians and others beyond count, standing together with our brothers and sisters for the total healing and restoration of this nation.

There were local businessmen who had left their places of work to be on their face at the altar. There were doctors, housewives, members of Parliament, military officials, government officers, soldiers, educators, musicians, worshippers, prayer warriors, children and many more. God gave the land a willingness to pray, a hunger for unity and an urgency to rebuild so that the latter glory of this land would be greater than the former. We repented. We tore down the altars of Baal and idolatry as Gideon did in Judges 6, in order to build in its place an altar to the Living God.

I came back to my room each night wiped out, poured out, depleted and exhausted but finding rest during each night which was deep and sound. This is how God totally refreshed our team day after day.

How can I describe what God did during those days? Can I measure heaven? How can I measure His glory, the depth of the work of the Spirit in countless hearts after binding the strongman in the heavens over a whole nation? While I cannot, the fruit will be the evidence.

As our teams watched, we were keenly reminded of our own prayer gathering in Gulu back in 2005 and how God defeated the enemy with obvious signs of wonders and miracles. God was on the move here as well and, once again, His power was stronger than that of the enemy. As we praised God for 10 years of peace in northern Uganda, we rejoiced for the way He had begun to replicate this work in the nation of South Sudan!

I knew, just like there, what He had begun, He would bring to completion, if we continued to press into Him for the fulfillment of His word and for "such a time as this!"

We had started the citywide, 40-day prayer and fasting chain, which led up to this particular prayer encounter in Juba, right about the same time as the 40-day Muslim feast of Ramadan ended. We were at the prayer altar, right in the heart of the city. Ramadan is a public holiday, celebrated worldwide and many of the Muslim opposition gathered alongside the open field where our prayer gathering was held. They began by bowing down and worshiping with their faces to the ground while slowly moving closer to our prayer gathering at the same time. It was done in open opposition to what God was doing. In spite of their loud, emotional prayers, their strongholds were weakening and they knew it. We prayed all the harder, binding the spirits of oppression, victimization and the antichrist. War took place in the heavens that day and just as God's people prayed like Daniel in Chapter 9, the Lord released the armies of heaven to come and do battle over the land. He Himself arose and His enemies were scattered! He arose with a righteous indignation when His people cried out and He came swiftly (Psa. 18) to repossess what was rightfully His.

The Muslim priests stopped praying after some time of spiritual battle in prayer on our part and moved back off the land. What a sign of victory over the powers of darkness!

Three times during our crusade, we prayed away black, angry clouds, full of lightning and loud thunder. If the rains had poured down on us, they would have soaked the event and collapsed our tents. It was in the middle of the rainy season and yet the Lord gave us the authority Jesus had in the boat when He spoke to the wind and the rain and calmed the storm. We stayed completely dry while the rains inundated the neighboring parts of the city.

It was on the last day, a gentle wind swept over the grounds. The prayer altar was almost full when the Lord opened heaven and gave us gentle, light showers. We danced in them and then knelt as a people rejoicing, dedicating the nation to the Lord again. Gentle showers here are a sign of God's blessings, His peace and His favor shining upon the land. I had wept like

Hosea 10:12, "Lord, please rain righteousness upon the land again, as we are on our faces, breaking up the fallow and hardened ground of our hearts and the heart of this nation." And the Lord did. Both physically and spiritually.

Leaders, bishops, pastors, intercessors, members of Parliament and strong, believing Christian soldiers, all stood up, one after the other, hour after hour, day after day, reading the Word, leading in prayer and testifying to God's goodness.

"This is the first time we have been drawn together as a land to seek the face of our God for a true II Chronicles 7:14 experience," they said. "This is the first time we have ever, in unity as a nation, built a prayer altar in our land to the Lord Jesus Christ; an altar of worship, of repentance, of sacrifice and of covenant. How grateful we are to God for using others in such a powerful way, to draw us together over tribalism, traditions, culture, bloodshed, hatred, revenge, murder, businesses and generational strongholds. It is the first time we have come as one body, one heart and one nation to be on our knees together, to seek the face of our one and only Savior. He is the only One who can save, forgive and restore and arise with healing in His wings." Their hearts were overflowing with overwhelming gratitude for what God, and God alone, was doing.

When the meetings were almost over, they pleaded with us, "Please don't stop here. We must continue to pray, to be united, to seek His face together and live in the new covenant that our Father has made with us and we with Him."

On the last day of our prayer gathering, I preached two services in Juba to English and Arabic speaking churches and poured my heart out with a passion beyond anything I had ever known. My message was called "Worshipers Take Down Giants." The Davidic anointing and the hearts of true worshipers was what God used to face the strongholds of darkness, defiance and evil over 'Goliaths' in order to deliver this nation. God confirmed His Word and poured out worship, deep, passionate, and transformational, as the congregation was on their knees, on their faces, standing or sitting, with each person pressing deeply into the very heart of God.

We left from that incredible service where God called us from "deep unto deep," and quickly drove back to the stadium for the last day of the prayer gathering. We arrived in time to find the people gathered and waiting to begin. It lasted for six more hours with no food, no break and no rest; yet energized with the power of heaven. I had asked God for a visible sign of His presence from this altar of prayer, as Elijah did when he stood before the prophets of Baal and called down fire from heaven, knowing God answers sacrifice with fire!

As we gathered in the field that day, one of our leaders received a call from one of the Honorable members of Parliament, who had joined us all week at this prayer altar.

"The peace talks in Addis Ababa will be signed in August." After two years of war, stalemate in battle and continued bloodshed and slaughter, what a wonderful answer to our prayers! It was truly news from heaven like the "fire upon the altar". We knelt, wept and rejoiced, asking the Father to now "seal that word" and let it come to pass. What a mighty and faithful God we serve!

God's presence was so heavy in the midst of us, no one wanted to move or leave. Oh, if we could have just stayed there forever and build our tents, as the disciples wanted to do when they stood on the Mount of Transfiguration with Jesus. Truly this had been a place of national transfiguration to bring in national transformation!

How wonderful if we could have "pitched our tents" and dwelt there. Instead, the Lord said, "No. Go down the mountain and begin to build, and I will restore the land. Begin to take the Gospel to the four corners of this nation, rebuilding My altars of prayer in every state. Reach out to every tribe and tongue in this land with the news of Jesus Christ and take it throughout the northern nations, where spiritual darkness reigns. I will give you the power to break their bondage and oppression with the powerful, liberating truth of My love. And don't stop until every tribe, every tongue and language has heard about Me. Go in My power and zeal, and freely give what you have freely received." (Matt. 24:14)

Chapter 16

In His Heavenly Royal Air Force

Can you imagine walking seven days in the blazing hot African sun, in over 100 degree-temperature, barefoot and with two children at your side? With little food or water, trudging on day after day, just to find the place where you heard there would be teaching about a man called "Jesus."

Susa did. She knew she had to get there and it didn't matter to her if she died on the way. What other hope did she have? Where else could she turn? She had heard a little announcement from the village radio, over the airwaves of the government station in the far northwest part of South Sudan, near the border of Darfur, about a crusade being held in Juba.

Her home had been in Sudan, where she was born to the tall, dark parents of the Dinka tribe, and had spent her life in hard rigorous work, digging in fields and trying to garden in the desert heat. Guns, bombs, air raids, with constant running and hiding in the bush had been her life since the day she was born.

When the nation of South Sudan was formed, she and her two sons were evicted from Sudan, the only home she had ever known. Forced to flee from Sudan to this new nation, she settled in a refugee camp in the Northern Bahr El Ghazal state. At that time, Favor of God Ministries was renting air time on a government radio station in Northern Bahr El Ghazal to announce the dates our team would be on the ground to share the truth and power of the Gospel.

The day Susa heard the news on the small village radio that Jesus was coming to be shared in the village, she determined in her heart she must go and meet this man who could change her life and give her hope. What else did she have for her children?

146

All they, too, had ever known was war, starvation, famine, hunger, gun fire and hiding.

Barefoot, with a little food and water for her journey with her two children, she made the seven-day journey by foot, to find the message of love, healing, and hope she had been promised. Yet when she and her two little boys arrived at the end of the last day of our seven-day crusade, we were in the midst of packing up. After a week of evangelism, door-to-door outreach, teaching, pastors' training and Bible distribution, our exhausted team was loading our vehicle and rented truck, eager to be on the road. We knew we had a hot, five-day journey back to Juba ahead of us over dusty, horrifically rugged and dangerous roads.

In that last hour, as our team loaded the last of our stuff, the three weary strangers stumbled into our camp. Worn and devastated, she had missed the whole week of meetings and teaching and felt she had lost her last strand of hope to ever meet this man called Jesus who could change her life. Exhausted, she fell to her knees sobbing. We embraced her, loved her and the children, and began to tell them the stories of Jesus. Her eyes lit up with hope as her heart embraced the truth. The smile that crossed her face was priceless as she and her sons knelt right there in the dirt with us and asked Jesus to come into their hearts.

What a dance there was in heaven that day! We rejoiced with her, fed her, gave her a Bible and led her to the nearest pastor to begin discipleship.

The delayed departure was worth the transfer of three more lives into the Kingdom of light! But that "divine delay" also saved our own lives on the road ahead of us. For later in the day, as we finally drove south in a caravan with the truck and land cruiser, the South Sudanese military pulled us off the road and said, "You can't go past this checkpoint. Pull over and find a place to sleep for the night. The cattle raiders have come with guns and there has been killing all along the roadside. If you had come any sooner, you would have driven right into the fight. They are waiting in ambush for the next travelers, but the South

Sudanese forces have come with reinforcement. We'll let you know when it's safe to continue."

The delay at the northern camp to lead Susa and her sons to Jesus kept us from driving right into the middle of an ambush and massacre along the road we were to travel. Praise God for His mercy!

What a story we had in our hearts on the way home, seeing Susa and her sons running into the embrace of a healing and loving Savior! It was worth it all.

As accounts of people hearing Favor of God on the radio once a week kept increasing, there began a stirring in my heart for our own radio station. So far, we were only renting a short time to announce the place for our crusades and other happenings with the ministry.

God began to show me that we had done well with portable Bible schools, crusades and other outreaches so far but there were many areas which were impossible for us to reach for the Gospel. Besides, there were not enough resources to send teams into the remote bush to preach the hope and love of Jesus to the many hungry souls like Susa.

Our ground troops had done well so far; now it was time for the Heavenly Royal Air Force to reach the far corners with His message through the airwaves, in places where no man had gone before.

But I still hesitated. It would involve us building a radio station. In my mind, I had not come here to build physical buildings as men do; but a spiritual Kingdom. The idea of getting involved in construction was alien to me as a woman and I could not get excited about it. Until the Lord brought it to me in a way which convinced me beyond a single bit of doubt.

For some reason, I was prompted to take a team to a government prison in a remote area called Patika; to take the Gospel to their prisoners. Our prison ministry had been extremely successful in Gulu and the surrounding areas and I felt led to reach out further.

We drove over narrow so-called "roads" with the grass on each side taller than the car, over rickety bridges, rocky creeks and sliding mud paths for hours on end. Each time we stopped to ask where the prison was, people simply pointed us further in the direction of a high mountain. Thinking the prison was at the foot of the mountain, we were astounded to find out it was way up at the top instead. There were moments we knew this was the end of us but we had to go on. There was no way to turn around on the narrow road winding its way up the steep incline.

When we finally arrived at our destination, it turned out the prison was actually in an old castle built by Idi Amin, the brutal ruler of many years ago. Prisoners in yellow clothing met us and motioned for us to enter the compound. From what it looked like, they were farming the land, growing vegetables and harvesting fruit to sustain themselves. As I looked around, I missed the usual monkeys and asked why there weren't any. They chuckled and I realized, over the years, they had killed them all for meat.

After showing us around the castle, we were allowed to sit on the throne once occupied by Idi Amin. It left me with the thought of how fleeting is man's power and how sad the end of evil. All that is left of this brutal dictator's legacy is a distasteful footnote in history.

After a while, the prisoners asked us to gather under a big tree, where I began to preach about the freedom of Christ and their need for His salvation. After a short time, several hands went up and I thought they were ready to accept Christ into their hearts.

Instead, through an interpreter, they asked,

"Are you the white lady on the radio?"

Puzzled, I replied, "I do preach on the radio once a week with Favor of God ministry but I don't think it reaches all the way up here."

"Favor of God!" they shouted. "We listen to you every week and have gotten saved and now hold Bible Studies. You have changed our lives."

It was in that instance I realized; we needed our own radio station since God seemed to say, 'Do you see what radio can do? It can go where you can't and raise up my people in areas you will never see and may never reach. This way My Word will go into even the remotest corner if you will be a part of My Royal Air Force.'

His words gripped me with deep conviction as I stood there and watched their shiny faces looking up at me. What if our very own radio station could send His message over the air waves every day and set a thousand prisoners and Susas free? What if she could have heard that news daily, in her own little village, with the community of refugees gathered around their camp fires every night as they always do, listening to the stories about Jesus on the one radio that belonged to the one person in the camp who owned one?

What if we could send the Truth over the airwaves, at an accelerated speed, to reach the "unreachable" people in those villages and tribes who have never heard the Gospel message?

It convinced me beyond a shadow of doubt, we must get the truth out over the airwaves and so become part of God's Royal Air Force.

Bullets and bombs can never stop it. Guns and evil can never shoot it down. Electricity or internet access could never shorten its reach. Lack of literacy could never stop it from entering thousands of hearts; bad roads or ambushes along treacherous terrain could never interfere with the message of freedom of God's love and truth! This could become one of the most powerful and fastest tools for transformation for most rural people, who don't read yet, don't have televisions, electricity or internet. But almost everyone has a radio! And everyone, from children to the elders, can hear truth and the transforming power of God's Word!

In wonder I realized, whether we were present or not, prisoners could be set free, thousands could come to the Light and truth could push back the deception and darkness! Children could be taught and won to Jesus at an early age! Men and women could learn about farming, families, health and healing for their hearts! They could learn how to worship, sing again and be restored to their purpose and destiny from the inside out. Why had it taken me this long to realize it?!

This vision for a Christian radio station was birthed in my heart on that mountain top, standing in the midst of those isolated prisoners in Idi Amin's castle. In His mercy, when God decided it was time to have a radio station, He showed me clearly in spite of my objections. Faith does not bear fruit when we do the logical thing but only when we do what He says to do, whether it seems logical or not. The Lord is a God of order and logic. The trouble is, it is His logic, not ours, He wants us to follow.

"For my thoughts are not your thoughts, neither are your ways my ways, says the Lord." (Isaiah 55:8)

In 2014 Favor FM 93.3 went on the air, bringing the message of salvation and healing to the Gulu area. Our team called it, 'The heartbeat of God'. What a name, as it reflected His deep passion for every human being. Though the equipment was old and rented, the Word of God was fresh and powerful. Listeners were calling in by the dozens daily with testimonies of healing and transformation and questions of discipleship! We were so grateful for each and every life! The next step would be to have our station reach all across Uganda and South Sudan in their very own language 24/7 in every village, any time of the day or night.

While few had internet or television, all radio needed was a tiny, single-battery or solar-powered transistor. For many, this was their only connection with civilization, the news, warnings of rebels, political insurgencies or advancing danger. They carried it with them in the fields as they worked, took it tied to bikes and motorcycles around town and played it in the market places as goods were sold. There was one sitting in the window of almost every little village hut. Students carried it in their pockets walking to school or laying it beside their beds at night while listening to worship, while the message of salvation filled their heart with peace, power and the presence of the Living Savior.

This amazing, seemingly insignificant tool had the potential to reach thousands in a day. In time, I was sure God wanted us to go further and reach the countries of Uganda, Sudan and Congo with His Royal Air Force, carrying not bombs, but His Word and reaching one soul at a time with the fire of His love.

One of our local pastors, Francisco, was preaching on the radio one evening, when in the midst of his message, the Holy Spirit prompted him to speak the following words, "Aber, Aber," he said, "Don't commit suicide. God has a plan for you. Aber, stop!" The airwaves went silent. Finally, Francisco found his place and continued preaching, moved and curious about this person named Aber. Would he ever find out?

Within an hour, Francisco had his answer. Aber, her husband and their two-month old baby arrived at the radio station. She explained that she and her husband had had a terrible argument because he had lost his job and it had been three days since they ate. With her last few shillings, she had gone to the pharmacy and picked up enough drugs to take her own life. As she was standing in the bathroom, ready to swallow them, she heard Pastor Francisco's voice over the radio. She instantly dropped the drugs, fell to her knees and began crying out to God. Her husband ran to her, took her in his arms and told her how sorry he was.

Pastor Francisco prayed for Aber and her husband and they both gave their lives to Jesus. God truly intervened in a dramatic, mysterious way by using our little radio station called Favor FM 93.3 Uganda to save Aber's life. We have had many divine interventions just like that since then over the airwaves and are grateful to the Lord for reaching out to His people in this simple, yet dramatically effective way.

Crusade in South Sudan
They turn in their wheelchair after being healed

Chapter 17

Jesus Works Miracles!
Come, Dead or Alive

My mother wrote a book called 'Penetrating the Strongholds of Islam'. When the Lord opened up for us to minister in Sudan, I realized her mantel had passed on to me. The Lord showed me there would be many doors of opportunity in the midst of countless adversaries.

My mother was a woman of strong faith, while my father was a man of prayer. However, it was my grandmother who told me so many years ago, "Honey, I'm passing on the baton to you." I had no idea what she meant as I sat with her in prayer during my visits. "I'm on the mountain with Jesus," she would tell me as she interceded, travailed and wept for an hour, sending "the Hound of Heaven" after the unsaved in her New York neighborhood. "Let's go fishing, Honey," she would tell me the next day as we walked through the streets, witnessing to everyone who passed by.

She had passed her unwavering faith on to my mother, who was a powerful woman, strong as steel in her faith and service to the Lord, while raising four of us in the deep jungles of the Philippines, assisting my father in the ministry in the midst of terrorism and war.

This all came back to me when Favor of God began to reach out into the Muslim strongholds of Northern Sudan. Nothing had changed. The need for breaking the strongholds of Islam and witchcraft was still as much the will of the Lord as it had been then. My grandmother's words, "Now it is your turn" came back to me as we were on the way to Rumbek, a town to the north-west of Juba, a four-to-five days' ride from Gulu.

When we arrived at Freedom Square, the place of the upcoming crusade, I saw a shrine on the side of the big open field.

"What is the shrine for?" I asked. My interpreter hesitated for a moment.

"This was the payment for this land," he finally said.

"What do you mean, payment?" I was confused.

"When the town wanted to buy this property, the witch doctors demanded as payment a beautiful young girl as a living sacrifice. The shrine was built as a memorial to her."

I realized we had our work cut out for us in the midst of this darkness and evil. But God would prevail! A lot goes into the preparations for a crusade and our team worked hard to distribute the fliers all across the area. Without a doubt, they generated a lot of attention with their message: JESUS IS COMING! COME DEAD OR ALIVE.

And they came – by the thousands! From the city, from the countryside and across the entire area they streamed into the Freedom Square. We knew there was no way we would be able to handle the masses. Our team felt overwhelmed and there was nothing to do but give them all to the Lord. He could and would handle it. And He did!

They brought them on stretchers and in chains, the sick and the mentally ill. They brought them walking on crutches and riding in wheelchairs, hundreds and hundreds of them as I preached the message of the healing blood of Jesus and His love for them. By the thousands they stretched out their hands receiving salvation when I presented the Gospel to them. And God came in a mighty way.

Before we could lay hands on anyone, there was a commotion in the front to the side of the podium. People were shouting and screaming when a man parted the crowd and ran away. We had no idea what had happened and continued with the meeting. It was the next day; the same man pushed himself through the crowd up to the platform.

"I want to testify!" he shouted. I waved him on and through a translator he told his story. "My name is Deng and I am from a village not too far from here. Do you remember the commotion from last night? My friends brought me here on a stretcher, because I have never walked since birth. I am thirty-five years old." He pointed to me, "When you told the story of the cripple at the pool at Bethesda who was healed by your Jesus, something stirred within my heart. When you said, this Jesus is the same yesterday, today and forever, I believed you and got up from my stretcher. My legs were healed and I ran back to my village to tell them about this. They killed a goat and we celebrated last night. Today, I brought everyone in the village to hear more about Him." He pointed to a group of about four hundred people in the crowd, who shouted and waved, rejoicing with him.

During the following days of the crusade, countless people were healed and set free from demonic bondage as the chains of the mentally ill were broken. The unusual thing about all this was, we never prayed for anyone, but only preached the Gospel. The Lord did the rest.

One day during the crusade, they brought a girl up front and laid her on the platform. When we walked over to her, we discovered she was dead! Immediately, the team laid hands on her and prayed; shouting and rebuking the spirit of death from her. After a while, she started breathing and sat up. She was very skinny and weak but she was definitely alive. I asked for her mother to come and take her and feed her some solid food. The next day her mother brought her back to let us know she was getting stronger. We made it possible for her daughter to go to school and lead a normal life. Today, she is a perfectly healthy girl.

Our next crusade was in Wau, the capitol city of South Sudan. It was the one city the Muslims had captured in order to use it as a platform to spread Islam into South Sudan. It was therefore a stronghold of Islam and the gateway to the purely Muslim nations in the North of Africa.

People all the way from Khartoum, the capitol city of North Sudan, had heard about our posters, which said, JESUS WORKS MIRACLES! COME, DEAD OR ALIVE.

With 1.2 million people attending, this turned out to be the largest crusade we had ever had. Government leaders counted the numbers and told us, since the crowds were so great, they blocked the roads and closed the whole town down. Once again, we knew God would have to show up and perform miracles, signs and wonders without us laying hands on anyone. The sight of that many people was overwhelming as we stood at the podium, awestruck, before this sea of humanity surrounding us.

There was a very wealthy Muslim lady who had traveled from Khartoum to Wau by plane to attend the crusade. She was carried in on a stretcher. Her hip socket was worn out to the point that her hip would not stay in place, even after several surgeries. As we were preaching on the resurrection power of Jesus Christ, I quoted the scripture from Romans 8:11, which says, "And if the Spirit of Him who raised Jesus from the dead is living in you, He who raised Christ from the dead will also give life to your mortal bodies through His Spirit, who lives in you."

At that moment, faith quickened her body and she shouted out loud, "I know it is mine! Healing is mine!" With that she rose up from her stretcher and, in her Burka, ran up and down, this way and that, until she ended up at the platform, sharing with us what had happened. "Allah couldn't do this, but Jesus did!"

Seeing what had happened, many of the Imams, who were at the meeting, came to the Lord. God was reaching out to the Muslims with signs, wonders and miracles and we were witnesses of His power.

It was in the 80's, when the church increased praying for Muslims on a worldwide scale. Since then, the Lord has appeared to many in dreams and visions and they now serve a God who is alive and has power to change lives. In this last decade, millions of Muslims have come to Jesus through signs, wonders and miracles and experience the reality of the Gospel. People want to serve a God who is alive and shows up with the kind of power they saw in these open-air meetings.

We held crusades in Torit, Rumbek and Wau that year; all with the same results of amazing signs, wonders and miracles, of salvations, healings and deliverance. These meetings were followed up by portable Bible schools and tremendous church growth. The Lord was truly penetrating into the heart of the enemy with His Word and His power, whether it be witchcraft or Islam. We were only the messengers, watching in awe and wonder, as His Spirit swept in and began to change a nation.

But the enemy was still very much alive. While there, I asked to be taken to the most powerful witch doctor in the area of Rumbek. A man came and got into our vehicle and led us into the bush country, far away from any town. On the way, every mile or so, we saw huts with a white flag in front, which showed there was a witch doctor in residence. This region was saturated with them. They had a tremendous hold over the population. Even men in suits could be seen dragging a goat or a cow to be sacrificed. I remembered the witch doctors in Gulu complaining we were destroying their livelihood with our Christianity, to which I answered them, "The Lord will provide something else."

There, as here, it was quite a business racket and whether they were successful or not, people continued to go to them when there was a problem.

After a long drive, we finally arrived at the mud hut of the most feared and powerful witch doctor in the area. She happened to be a lady. As we pulled up to the side of her hut, we saw a group of people sitting in a circle with a young girl in their midst. We realized they were in the middle of a ritual. We started praying under our breath immediately and didn't dare move closer for fear of losing our lives. We had heard this lady had the reputation of killing at the slightest provocation.

She was dressed in a black robe and I noticed one of her eyes was missing. Four or five men, clad only in a G-string, their bodies painted in vivid colors and holding long spears, danced around her. Apparently, according to our guide, the family had asked them to put a curse on a man who had hurt their daughter.

Suddenly, the men grabbed several chickens and then a goat and slit their throats. They held the dead animals above the girl, allowing the blood to flow over her head and down her body, until she was covered with it, all the while screaming and screeching in the most piercing wails and chants.

I had a hard time to keep from vomiting at this gruesome spectacle, but did not dare move. When the ritual was over, I stepped up to the group and asked, "We are visitors and have something to say. Could you all sit down for a minute, please?"

Apparently, the witch doctor thought we were prospective customers and nodded her head for us to speak. She was sitting in the middle, surrounded by the men with the spears.

"I have come to share with you about the blood of Jesus. When He died for our sins on the cross, He did away with blood sacrifice once and for all. He wants to set you free from the curses of Satan if you turn your life over to Him."

After about five minutes of this, the woman became very agitated and jumped up screaming in her dialect, "The demons are leaving me and my power has gone!" With that she ran into her mud hut, only to appear after a short while, stark naked, a wild look in her eye. She pointed at us and yelled to the men with the spears, "Go get them!"

Without hesitating, we ran to our car and sped off before they could get to us. No doubt they would have killed us all.

The power of Satan is still very real in many of these African countries, even today. One of the reasons is that no foundation of godliness has ever been laid over many generations in these regions. While they have had revivals and missionaries over the years, none have been able to fully transform and renew the minds of the people because they were either driven out, killed or died from dangers and diseases. Could it be, they did not know about the power of God to defeat the enemy and relied on their own strength instead? And maybe as a result, they not only lost their ministry, but even their lives?

As Christians, on our own we do not have the power or strength to defeat the darkness of the enemy but must rely on the Name of Jesus and His Holy Spirit in order to win the battle. And the battle for Africa is still raging. What was only the occult before, has now joined forces with Islam and even Communism. Christianity without God's power is no match for either one or the forces of darkness. It takes the infilling and empowering of the Spirit of God in us if we want to win over these nations for Jesus and spread the truth of the living God who sent His Son Jesus to die for them. My life has certainly been an example. One lonely, white woman, sent where no one wanted to go, was all the Lord needed to begin the defeat of an enemy who had choked these people for decades through horror, witchcraft and endless, murderous wars. To walk into these kinds of strongholds in my own power would have been suicide; but to enter in the Name of Jesus has meant victory. We serve a mighty God!

'To take a land and occupy' was made real when God showed me to build church buildings in the villages which had turned to the Lord. I was reluctant because there was nothing mentioned in the book of Acts about building anything other than people to raise up the Temple of the Holy Spirit within each believer.

"How come there is a mosque being built in almost every town but the children of God have to meet in mud huts?" I was asked by many of the villagers. Just like the idea of the radio station, the Lord had to show me, through a special incident, how wrong I had been with this idea.

It started when one of our partners in the US called me to let me know it was the mandate of his ministry to blanket the nations with church buildings.

"How many can you build?" I asked him, expecting a low number.

"As many as you want," he said without hesitation.

"How about a thousand in Northern Uganda," I answered, almost as a joke.

"Ok, we'll do it," he answered.

"Can you build another thousand in South Sudan?" I asked, holding my breath.

"Sure."

I was speechless. The Lord had once again showed me He was able to provide in spite of my unbelief.

We started building as soon as the funds arrived, when one of our team leaders came to me with a request.

"My parents live in Atiak and have heard about Favor of God building church buildings. My father went through horrible times with the LRA rebels with countless murders and brutalities for many years. He owns a piece of land in our village and has decided he wants to dedicate that blood-soaked place for the first church building as a monument to the Living God. He insists his community now belongs to Jesus and the church will be an outward sign to everyone."

I met Loum and his wife Mama Delfina. They had turned their lives over to the Lord not too long ago and worked tirelessly to spread the Gospel. During the construction of the church, the entire village got involved and was transformed in the process. People came from miles around for the dedication service, and later I had the honor to preach there.

Not long after, a witchdoctor decided she wanted to move back into the village. In a united front, the people told her, "God lives here now; no more witch doctors. Either you get saved or get out!"

When I heard about this, I realized their church building was not just a matter of mud and brick but had become a tabernacle of the Living God for the villagers. Dedicated to Him, it served as a visible reminder of His presence for His people, just as the temple of Jerusalem had been for the Jews.

All of these small buildings going up around the nation are now also used for training, teaching and instruction in daily skills for women and empower them to feed and educate their families by teaching them to raise pigs, chickens and other livestock. Financial management was another area, as well as equipping them to begin their own small business ventures and take them from "aid" to "trade". This empowerment not only built their family's economic situation, but served to increase their confidence in themselves to learn self-worth and purpose. Nursery schools take place during the week in many of these churches, from Monday through Friday, teaching children in academics and Bible.

This "building boom" is still in progress and I have no doubt the Lord will continue to bless it until a thousand new church buildings have been built in both Uganda and South Sudan. The Kingdom of God is on the move, not just in the spiritual realm, but also in the form of brick and mortar until the Lord returns for His Bride. There is no doubt in my mind His Spirit will be victorious over the enemy, not just in Africa, but across the nations if we are faithful to "go into all the world and preach the Gospel". I invite you, the reader, to join me and become a soldier in His Army, whether on the ground or in the air, with prayer or finances in order to fulfill His Great commission.

The next week, as I was on my face in the House of Prayer with our team in Gulu, during morning devotions, the Lord spoke to my heart and said, "You've been through bullets and buildings, but now I'm going to use you for babies." I knew this meant the spiritual birthing of a new harvest into His family, more than any of us could ever count.

No one knows what the future has in store for any of us. All we can do is stand together as workers in God's vineyard and so fulfill the purpose the Lord has for us, each in our designated place, to bring in His rich harvest.

It is my greatest desire that I have been able to share with you His power in raising up a people, who were not His people, and help them to become His glorious Bride. To think He wants to use all of us in spite of our unworthiness is simply too wonderful to comprehend. Together, we can stand shoulder to shoulder in His Army until the day He returns and tells us, "Well done, my good and faithful servants."

Will you join me on the frontlines?

Chapter 18

Others Are Moving Out
We Are Moving In

The frontlines of the real battle have nothing to do with people, politics, parties or even countries. It is a worldwide clash between Islam and Christianity and cannot be won with armies or ordinary weapons of warfare. It is a clash of the titans in the spiritual realm, the age-old battle between God and the satanic forces of evil.

This end-time clash heated up when secular humanism took hold in the sixties and met with a spirit of apathy within the church. It was an unseen, shadowy enemy, without outward form or substance, yet it invaded many western societies first, and then the church. This same enemy, just in a different form, has now come out of the shadows and is taking the world by storm. And now, as the church is blinded by the enemy of secular humanism and situational ethics, the last of the giants has entered in on its back. Its name is Islam. It makes no secret of its goal of world dominion and the destruction of Judaism and Christianity.

All this, while the church and the western nations are in an almost comatose slumber of apathy and ignorance. Apathy has watched silently as God is evicted from our government and institutions through political correctness and the law. Ignorance stems from lack of knowledge of the Word of God, resulting in the erroneous belief Allah and the true God are one and the same. This is widely accepted not just in our society, but across many of the denominational churches. Christianity and Islam are joining forces together in many worldwide arenas and is touted as 'Chrislam'. It could be seen as the platform for the Antichrist and the one world government to come.

'My people are destroyed from lack of knowledge. Because you have rejected knowledge, I also reject you as my priests; because you have ignored the law of your God, I will also ignore your children.' Hosea 4:6

And we wonder why so many of our younger generation are turning away from God.

The western church needs to wake up from its slumber and join in the fight against this powerful enemy. God has given us Christians the spiritual weapons of warfare to defeat this invasion, not by human means, but by taking up the armor of God in the Name of Jesus.

I traveled in the US through most of 2016, because I had been asked to teach and pray with committed Christians against this enemy during the Election, in order to move God's hand and return our nation back to godly principles. Having dealt with satanic forces for so long in northern Uganda and South Sudan, as well as growing up in a Muslim village in the Philippines, I was seen as somewhat of an authority on standing against the forces of Satan. While I found many people oblivious to this spiritual battle, there were just as many who discerned correctly what was going on. With Christianity under attack and Muslim prayer being accepted and actually encouraged on the steps of the White House, these things were hard to ignore. We knew if God did not intervene on His people's behalf, America, as we knew it, would not survive. To the total surprise of the world, He did perform a miracle on Election Day and pulled our country back from the abyss. Praise God!

When I returned to Uganda, in the beginning of 2017, I immediately chose to go on to South Sudan, where the situation was so bad, the authorities had told all foreigners to leave.

"That is not possible," I answered them. "We are going in to establish the Kingdom in the power of the living God." Once again, I had no idea how we would go about this in the midst of the vicious, armed conflict going on in this nation. I decided, as long as the Lord was not worried, neither would I be.

"That is not possible," they told me. "Foreigners are advised not to go. It is too dangerous."

In spite of their warning, I put one of the houses we had purchased up for sale to have enough funds to look for a more centrally located mission base in Juba, the capital of South Sudan. The economy at the time was at a point where it was pretty well impossible to find a buyer. In spite of it, the Lord sold the house so we could have the funds to look for a ministry center right in the heart of the city; for the radio, house of prayer and a continuous prayer altar for the salvation of the nation.

The day before I and my good friend Martha were to leave, I got violently ill with some sort of food poisoning. I did remember I had not washed my hands thoroughly enough at a meeting we had the day before. There was no way to go now, but to wait till the next morning until we headed out.

When we got across the border of South Sudan, just on the other side, we stopped at a Christian training camp.

"Thank God you didn't come yesterday," they told us. "There was an all-out bloody battle between a rebel group and government soldiers where several people got killed. You would have been right in the middle of that had you left when you wanted to." Once again, God had spared me by a divine delay; using something as ordinary as vomiting all day to keep me from getting killed.

Once we entered South Sudan, we were accompanied on our trip by a military escort made up of one tank, three trucks and thirty to forty South Sudanese soldiers, fully armed with AK47's, to keep us safe. The roads were eerily empty as we made our way to Juba.

"Martha, read the Bible," I said as we drove down the dirt roads. "Don't stop until we get there because the tanks and soldiers can't do what the Word of God can. It is our only protection."

When we finally arrived in Juba, the people cried, "You

came through danger, shooting and killing to be with us," they said. "God alone could have kept you safe. Now we know how much you love us and this nation. To think you risked your lives to come and bring us prayer and the Word of God."

"The Apostle Paul was not guided by bad news, but by the Holy Spirit, who told him when to go and when not to," I answered. "God has blocked every hindrance and, because of His divine intervention, we were saved."

Our Military Escort

Driving through the large city of Juba the next day, we realized we would need a House of Prayer in the center of the town in order to advance the Kingdom in this place.

"Where are we going to find a building, centrally located and big enough, yet affordable, for a House of Prayer?" I asked Martha. "Unless God provides, there is no way we have the funds for even the most modest place."

It was at that moment we drove by an empty warehouse.

"Let's find out how much they want for it," Martha said. "This is exactly what we need."

People had warned us that a piece of property in Juba city

would cost at least $5 million USD! It turned out, the owner miraculously wanted a much less amount than that but it was still totally out of reach for us, given the fact, as usual, we didn't have a penny at that moment. Besides, the place had no electricity, no running water or any other conveniences.

"Other than that, it is perfect," I said as we drove off. "Right downtown, the right size, with enough office space for the radio. The warehouse would make a perfect house of prayer and it's even near the Juba University. Only God can make this happen."

That February, in 2017, Daddy Ray, an eighty-year-old man from Australia let me know he was coming to visit. He was a wonderful, mighty man of God, who had served the Lord for many years in Africa.

"God has kept me alive through many surgeries so I can come and minister with you in South Sudan at this time," he announced with great joy.

Immediately, I began organizing a large conference in Juba for pastors, leaders, government officials and businessmen to hear this wonderful servant of God. And they came. What a sight it was to see these men of God, some three hundred leaders, along with chaplains in uniform, dancing and singing to the Lord. There were even Episcopal and Catholic clergy as well as Baptists and other intercessors, as Daddy Ray turned the place upside down, ministering to them in his own special, anointed way.

Favor of God teams offered free training and gave out over two hundred Bibles to Parliament officials. They wept as they took them and said, "We have to have God in government if this country is going to be healed."

Daddy Ray teaching us

It seems they meant what they said because the following March the government called for a National Prayer Conference to which I was invited.

Before that, we decided to rent a large church to house more of these conferences to establish the daily House of Prayer meetings, when several brokers from Juba called us. "We think we have the right place for what you are looking for," they said. "It's not for rent, but we think we can make arrangements for a small down payment for you to buy it."

They took us to the very warehouse Martha and I had looked at several months ago! God had vacated it for us and made it possible so it could be our first House of Prayer and Radio station in South Sudan! We were even allowed to renovate it before we made the first down payment. When it was done, it had a good-sized hall, a bedroom for me and one for staff, two rooms for the radio station and two rooms for offices.

The grand-opening was held in May with elaborate festivities to which the city was invited. The hall was filled with believers and visitors praising and worshiping the Lord for this miracle.

We gave away audio and written Bibles to saturate the darkness with the light of the Gospel.

We told those who came, "Go! Run with it and cover the land with God's message. Turn on the light in the midst of the deepest darkness."

While there, I met with many believers who were refugees from Darfur, a region in the northwest of Sudan. During a pastors' training, one of their leaders, Pastor Rico, shared his dramatic story of how the Lord 'recruited' him to serve the believers who had fled the ravages of persecution by Islam in the Darfur area. Spellbound, we listened to him as he shared how he found Jesus in a most unusual, dramatic way.

"I grew up in a Muslim home, as did all the children in Darfur, for anyone found to be of any other religion was imprisoned or put to death. As I studied and prayed hard with the other Muslim children my age, I began to question the Koran.

"This doesn't make sense and cannot be true," I told my teachers. They became angry with me and told me, "Be careful, you can be arrested."

But I kept questioning and openly challenging the Koran at the University in Nyala, the capital of Darfur. I openly argued that the Koran was a lie. I challenged my teachers, "I know this isn't true, it can't be. It doesn't even line up with itself from one part to the other." They became furious with me as I refused to believe their explanations. As a result, they had me picked up by the military and imprisoned. In prison, I was beaten severely and told never to question the Koran again. I was released after 30 days and resumed my studies, still convinced it was a lie. I was going to give my life to believe it to be so and knew I must find the truth.

Again, I was arrested. This time for 6 months. Once again, I was beaten, but it didn't make me stay quiet or back down. I couldn't understand the hate and violence in this system of Islam.

Upon release, I went back to the University and began to question and challenge my professors and colleagues publicly about the truth of the Koran.

Again, I was taken to prison, and this time sentenced to severe torture, and even death, but I still refused to repent for my doubts. I didn't even understand why, except for a deep feeling in my heart the real truth was somewhere for me to find; and continued to speak about this openly, even from prison.

Until finally, I was sentenced to be executed.

The day before my execution, one of the guards came to me and said, "You used to teach school to my children in my village and helped my family one time when we were in need. We are going to get you out of here."

Secretly, he bought me an airline ticket to Khartoum and then released me. He even took me to the airport and to freedom.

When I reached Khartoum, with nothing in hand, and no job, I found the people there also loved and stood on the Koran. I didn't want to risk my life again for denying this book, so I decided to migrate south, where I heard that some of the people there, in South Sudan, also opposed the Koran and its doctrines.

There I found the dark-skinned Sudanese people, just like myself and joined their Sudanese People's Liberation Movement, which was their South Sudan military forces, and was known as the army of the nation. They didn't care if I was from the north or the south of Sudan, as long as I was willing to fight for their cause to overthrow the dark and hateful oppression of the Islam regime which had taken control of northern Sudan. I decided to join them in their fight for liberty.

It was during a battle in a village, when I saw a little church packed with people praying fervently. I was amazed at the faith and love of these Sudanese believers, who began talking to me about a man named Jesus, who came to die for me, because He loved me.

They offered to pray for me, and knowing I didn't want the Koran, I decided then and there to receive this Jesus they were talking about. Somehow, I knew in my heart He was the One I had been searching for and the truth I had been longing to find.

The little church where people prayed

When the southern part of Sudan gained their independence in 2011, I was finished fighting. That is when I began to study the Christian faith. I found other Darfurians who had received Jesus and had fled from our state in Sudan to South Sudan, where they found refuge and the chance to worship freely.

We joined together, speaking the same mother dialect, and began a home fellowship group, which now has grown into a church. When South Sudanese Muslims discovered me, they threatened to kill me several times. Yet I was spared because they later realized I had fought in the SPLM army. I therefore became a threat to them and they left me alone. As our fellowship grew, I was asked to pastor this refugee group of Darfurians in Juba.

Here we are today, believing with all our hearts as 70 believers who have banded together, knowing that God raised us up to go back into our dangerous state and take the Gospel, do or die. By now, we have begun training and have already sent four believers there for six months mission work. They will return and we'll send the next four.

All this is underground work and they can't stay longer than about six months for fear of discovery.

In spite of the danger, the Holy Spirit continues to guide our efforts through signs, wonders and miracles. Since then, we have seen whole villages saved as our people are guided by divine intervention to go to certain houses, where people are waiting for them,

"Where have you been, we have been waiting for you to come," they say, with thirty to fifty Muslims waiting in each hut for us when we arrive. The Holy Spirit directs us to exactly the right village and the right house, and there these people are, all dressed in their Muslim attire, waiting for us to share the Gospel. Mind you, these are not Christians, but Muslims, promised through dreams and visions "someone will come and direct you to the truth in your own language". By the time we get there, they are ready to accept Jesus into their hearts the moment they hear the message of salvation and are eager to be baptized.

Our missionaries are smuggled over the border, hiding in gunnysacks to reach these spiritually hungry people, ready to give their lives to carry the Gospel to the equally hungry in Darfur. Some of them walk through swamps, fighting snakes for three days to cross secretly back into our own nation with the message of the truth and carrying as many Bibles as they can. They know it is not organized religion that will turn this country around; only Jesus. They are on fire and fearless and are convinced "We will win the Muslim world to Jesus."

These evangelists are as fearless as ISIS and tell us, "If they can be that committed, why shouldn't we?"

When I asked some of them in prison about it, they answered, "Why wouldn't we be? Our eternity is secure, theirs isn't. Why wouldn't we give one life to save many?"

Pastor Rico closed his story with this plea, "We need help desperately. We need to train them and send them with Arabic Bibles to take into Darfur. We also need to take care of our refugee families who are here in South Sudan and to equip our church so it can become an equipping and sending station. Will you help?"

When he was done, he turned to me and said, "Carole, I love your vision and the Favor mission team. We have connected to you in heart because we know we can never fulfill this calling alone. Since God has already placed our nations on your heart, I know we can be stronger in fulfilling this mission together."

"I want to go with you," I answered spontaneously. "For many years I have told God I am ready to die taking the Gospel into the 10/40 window if He asks me to."

"You cannot go, Carole, because you would be too conspicuous in my country, putting our people in great jeopardy."

"Then Favor of God Ministry will stand with you, empower your people, help equip them and send them in any way we can," I said with great conviction.

That evening in prayer, God confirmed what I had told him with these words, 'Some I have called to die for Me, while others are called to live for the increase of My Kingdom. You, Carole, I have called to send them in My Name.'

Chapter 19

A Mighty Force

"Everyone who calls on the name of the Lord will be saved. How, then, can they call on the one they have not believed in? And how can they believe in the one of whom they have not heard? And how can they hear without someone preaching to them? And how can they preach unless they are sent? As it is written, "How beautiful are the feet of those who bring good news!" Romans 10:13-15

For so many years, western missionaries were the only ones to spread the Gospel in Africa. God's mandate "to go into all the world" was meant for everyone who calls on the name of the Lord. The Lord impressed me early on, I was not only to bring the message of salvation to Africa, but rather go further and make disciples of all nations. That is what Jesus told His disciples to do and that is what He burdened my heart to do. Converts are not the ones to bring in the harvest; disciples are.

Favor of God was there to raise an African army, empowered by the Spirit of God and equipped with His Word to spread His good news across the land by training second and third level trainers to be sent out to collect the harvest, ripe for the picking. Anyone who has ever been a farmer knows, a harvest not gathered on time will rot in the field and be lost. The fields of Africa not harvested for Jesus, will continue to be used by Satan and his forces through violence, war, murder and destruction. No human army can stand against him. No guns will defeat the demonic power of the enemy and no amount of money will change the hearts and minds of the millions of African people, who are tired of the bloodshed and horror across their land.

Neither can one man or woman do even a fraction of this alone. But an indigenous army, called by the living God, empowered with His truth, spreading out across these lands and carrying the message of salvation, can. Through His power and with one voice they can reach into the most remote and unreached villages and take Jesus to those gripped in darkness and fear, perishing for lack of knowledge.

Favor of God Ministry is equipping this mighty force of African missionaries, training them in the Word to go out fearlessly with wisdom, power and the zeal of the Lord. Equipped after going through two months of our portable Bible discipleship program, and some of them continuing onto Bible school, they are led by the Spirit to go into the most rural and remote villages throughout Northern Uganda and South Sudan.

To think western missionaries alone could possibly fulfill this assignment is unthinkable. It takes as much money to send out one western missionary as it does forty African ones. Besides, the indigenous believers are infinitely more effective because they speak the language, know the culture and the generational customs of the land. These soldiers of the living God have lived with nothing, know how to make do with very little and can relate to the problems and hopes of those to whom they preach. They have felt the darkness, hopelessness and terror of the endless wars and can now testify to the liberating power of Jesus Christ first hand.

By "the word of their testimony" they share the Gospel to their own people with zeal, power and a radical boldness that cannot be matched by those from the west, no matter how well-meaning we are. Like in the book of Acts, they do not need buildings and structures to preach the Gospel, but simply a large tree or dusty field will do to gather large crowds, just like Jesus did.

Favor of God has trained over 7,000 people using the Portable Bible School program and over 60,000 Bibles have been given out to people all over the North. Just like Jesus, to spread His message, He did not need a building of any kind, but a simple place where people gathered to listen to the Word of God. These training schools take about fifty to a hundred people in each village, for two months, train them in the Word of God, teach them how to teach it to others and then go from door to door to share the Gospel. Usually, out of those hundred, twenty-five start a new church in their area. If they bring only two people a week to the Lord, and those in turn do the same, and so on, within a year 2,600 more people have turned their lives over to Jesus. This is a simple example of accelerated harvesting and reaching into the most remote areas of Africa with the Gospel at an amazing rate of success.

One of those disciples we sent out, Owot, came back with an amazing tale of what drastic measures God will use to turn even the most unlikely sinner around to accept Jesus.

"I was preaching in this village and many people came to the Lord. The believers there were in the process of building a new church and everyone was filled with joy and excitement. However, there was one witch doctor among the people who persecuted the Christians and had even killed some. Everyone was afraid of her. One man in her village got so upset with her, he took a knife one evening and threatened to kill her. Screaming in fear, she ran to the new church and fell to her knees, calling on Jesus between sobs. We prayed for her and she repented of her witchcraft and accepted Christ as her Savior. The next day, when the villagers heard what had happened, almost everyone became a believer. "

While her neighbor should not have acted the way he did, God nevertheless used even his wrong actions to bring this woman to the Lord.

When I asked God to send me where no one wants to go, He took me at my word. Only one out of ten missionaries go into places where no one has preached before. Every great work has its genesis moment. Every powerful movement of God began in someone's prayer closet. Our Rural Education and Empowerment Program was no exception. Its genesis moment was in a rented room as I and a small group of Ugandans met daily to pray. And as we prayed, a burning desire to take the Gospel into the rural and remote villages of Northern Uganda was born in our hearts.

The first thirty-two graduates trained in our Gulu Bible school became the leaders of portable Bible schools, equipping and sending others with the goal to reach into the bush, the villages, the camps, the jungles, the rural churches and the most remote and unreached places on the map. This was our goal: Everyone must hear about Jesus! (Romans 10:14-15)

Within the first five years, we had discipled and equipped over 5,000 people for leadership through two months of intensive discipleship in our portable Bible school with practical experience in church planting, prayer, children's work and youth ministries. Over 40,000 Bibles in more than twelve languages were distributed. Trauma rehabilitation multiplied to over 36,000 hurting people, which were helped with deep emotional wounds left by years of war.

During this time, countless churches were planted, new converts baptized as existing churches grew in villages and in the bush. The hunger for the Word spread faster than it could be satisfied.

This was all made possible by God because hearts wept in prayer for the lost from the very first day in that little prayer room in Gulu, willing to sacrifice in secret. We were now seeing open rewards. God is the God of the impossible and His power was made manifest when we obeyed Him and went where no one wanted to go.

It is not just obedience God uses when He wants to fulfill our purpose – it is prayer. It alone brings the power of the living God in a mighty, miraculous way to change, create and rebuild His Kingdom, whether in America or Africa.

Have you ever asked yourself this question? "What would have happened differently if I had only prayed more?"

It brings to mind Jesus' question to the disciples, "Could you not even pray with me for one hour?" He asked that same question several times, and yet each time, found them sleeping. (par. Mark 14:37-42) Was He disappointed? Jesus knew His power and victory came from His Father through a close connection through prayer and kept alive by spending time with Him. How He wanted to share that kind of close communion and even suffering with His disciples because it was the only way for them to gain His strength, victory and power.

Andrew Murray quoted years ago, "We are no greater than our prayer life." We are only what we are in the secret place with the Father, no matter how shiny and spiritual we sound or act on the outside. It is God who sees the real us and judges our true spiritual state according to the hidden condition of our heart. He is the One who would ask you today:

Would you pray if you believed children's lives could be saved?

Would you pray if you believed we could have Bibles instead of bullets back in our schools again?

Would it be worth it to you to tarry with Him for one hour?

Would you pray if you believed in the real power of prayer that could shape history and turn the tide of events in the world or your country?

Would you be willing to take the time to agree with the heart of God for His purpose to be accomplished in the earth?

II Chronicles 7:14, so commonly quoted, begins with "IF". God has put a condition on the healing of our land and situations in our lives. It is in the "IF". His love is unconditional, and His mercy is new every morning. His faithfulness beyond measure, and His Word and character never change.

But He still put a condition in this verse on what is possible, if we would pray... Deuteronomy 28:1 also begins with "IF...we will listen and obey...I John 1:9, "IF" we confess our sins, He is faithful..."

He has given us a free choice and a will… to pray or not to pray, to ask or not to ask, to seek Him with our whole hearts or not to seek Him…

Choose today whom you will serve. And what you choose, do it with your whole heart. What God made possible over the many years I have served in Uganda, South Sudan and the surrounding regions, it was done because of fervent, consistent prayer. This kind of communion did not bring God closer to me and my team, it brought us closer to Him and made us realize our total dependence on Him. I know, beyond a shadow of doubt, it was His mercy and goodness which reached out to a land forsaken. It was His love and kindness that is turning Uganda and South Sudan from an abandoned slave into His beautiful bride.

How blessed I am to be a part of that transformation!

Chapter 20

His Light in the Darkness

A Word from Barbara

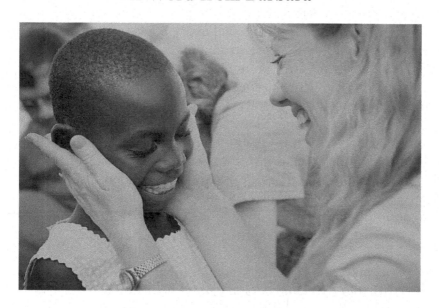

As you have read Carole's story, I hope you are amazed and filled with renewed faith in a God who is very much alive and active in the lives of those who not only hear His voice, but also do what it says.

It has been an honor to recount for you the astounding signs, wonders and miracles of this wonderful God, who sent His Son, not just for us, but for a people in a far away, forgotten land, ruled by evil and demonic powers. Our Jesus is still the Lion of Judah, and with this story, He wants to remind you, the battle in

181

the heavenlies is still raging over the souls of the lost, and yet, the victory has been won by Him on the cross.

My heart was stirred as I recounted for you how the Name of Jesus is still stronger than Satan's forces and His power to overcome obstacles of hate, violence and even death is not diminished. Many of you who read this story may have forgotten that we have authority over the enemy, not just in the bush country of Africa, but in the jungle of the West as well. You may even feel a little guilty that you are glad you were born into a place of abundance, instead of the violence and poverty of Uganda and South Sudan.

Yet there are many of us who feel every bit as spiritually starved in our comfortable, safe surroundings as the villagers were in Uganda when Carole brought them the Good News. There is only one difference between us and them: We are starving because we do not **believe** what God says. They were starving because they did not **know** what God says.

Our "spiritual diet" is made up of a mixture of doubt and human logic and the absence of solid meat, which is the Word of God. Add to that the rare times we spend a few moments with the Lord, and it explains our lack of faith as we helplessly watch our country fall into the abyss of unbelief. We have learned to listen to the enemy more readily than to the promises of our living Savior.

In our country, filled with abundant blessings and material riches, we are told the Name of God cannot be mentioned or displayed on any government monument, nor are our children able to pray in schools and universities because it is against the law. At the same time, our youth are indoctrinated in immorality and godlessness, and many of our churches preach a watered-down gospel while trying to blend in with other beliefs. A nation without God makes room for the same satanic forces which have ruled Africa for so long. Make no mistake, what Satan has done there, he will do in America if we do not stand against this flood of evil.

In writing Carole's story, I came to realize, the driving force of God's power and His blessings is in direct proportion to the amount of time we spend with Him in fervent prayer. Our fellowship and close relationship with the Lord alone helps bring about His will and purpose in our lives. While this does not bring God closer to us, it does draw us closer to Him, as it tells us in James 4:8 'Draw near to God and He will draw near to you.' Neither does it mean He will hear us better, but that we will hear Him more clearly.

This is demonstrated clearly in Carole's life and ministry, where God chose her to help raise the Ugandan and South Sudanese people out of the ashes of war and satanic oppression. Molded through the fires of adversity and hardship they were a ready harvest to become His shining Bride.

I stand amazed how He accomplished this with only one obedient woman, willing to go where no one wanted to go. It was as if He put one little, insignificant candle into a dark room, knowing, its small light could not be missed. When He sent Carole to Northern Uganda, one lone, white woman in a sea of dark faces, neither could she be ignored. Not because she was white, but because she was filled with HIS LIGHT.

However, from the start, God showed her that her ministry was not to be a one-woman show but rather a team effort with the motto 'If you want to go fast, go alone. If you want to go far, go together'. And so, she raised up an army of youth, a group of fearless giants of faith, who she trained to run with the Favor of God and His calling to the point, if anything were to happen to her, the ministry would go on. With these mighty men and women of God, who are filled with zeal in their dedication to Jesus and ready to offer themselves in the service of their people, Carole has been able to pass on this Light to the next generation. The reason for her remarkable success is, she made her ministry not about herself, but about God's power and the people she came to serve.

It is her greatest desire to pass that same light on to you, the reader. While she does not expect you to go to Africa, she wants to empower you to be a part of the Lord's work in His vineyard, wherever that may be.

I pray my account of God's mighty power will embolden you to see it is not **if** He wants to use you, but rather where and when. For He is ready to do the same miracles He performed in Uganda and South Sudan in your neighborhood, church or workplace, if you spend the time with Him to find out His will and purpose for your life.

Allow Him to use you by stepping out of the boat. It can be scary to trust Him, especially if all you see is water. Yet how exciting when you experience the solid ground He prepared for you before you were born, when you trust Him, one step at a time!

He is looking for water walkers to help those who are living and serving in the kind of faith Carole and her team operate. To be inspired by the miracles in this book is one thing, to translate that inspiration into action, is quite another. Carole can only go if you go with her, and together, fulfill His great mission – HIS Commission.

In spite of the wonderful results of thousands of souls brought to the Lord during these last few years, Islam is on an aggressive march into South Sudan. With it have come renewed unrest, war and bloodshed. If it succeeds, not only will the growth of Christianity be driven underground, but the church there will be persecuted by Islam, allowing it to spread unhindered to the countries of Central Africa. At this writing, Mosques are being built everywhere. Even if they are not used, they serve as storage areas for ammunition. Muslim schools offer a one-month salary to any parent who will send their children to be indoctrinated to worship and pray to Allah.

Once again, guns and wars will not stop this march of Satan, but the power and love of God will. Against all odds, Favor of God teams are still going forth into the North, all for the sake of taking Jesus to the unreached and to the Muslim world. In order to stem the tide of this flood, it will take the combined effort of the Army of God, which includes you, the reader, through your fervent prayer and financial support for Carole's teams. An army cannot fight without weapons. The weapons of Favor of God come from God's power and your generosity and faithfulness through praying and giving.

Will you stand with Carole and her eighty-member team and lift them up daily in fervent, passionate intercession?

Pray that her life and that of the team will be spared to continue this great work.

Pray for the ministry to reach those who are spiritually hungry and thirsty for the living Word of God.

Will you ask Him to protect the villages across the land from the enemy's attack?

Will you intercede for the churches in Uganda and South Sudan that they might be able to stand against the advancing forces of Satan?

Will you ask God to send His Holy Spirit to empower His Army to spread the Good News across the land by continuing to back it up with signs, wonders and miracles?

Most of all, will you pray for the advancement of the church into every corner of this territory and take it with the powerful force of the love of Jesus?

Read on the next page how you can become part of Carole's ministry by stepping out of the boat.

After praying, the second, most important way you can be a part of this ministry is by becoming a regular partner with Favour Africa. Your small or large one time or monthly contribution will enable Carole to continue and advance the work the Lord has started in Uganda and South Sudan.

If you decide to become a partner to bring in the harvest in Uganda and South Sudan, go to our website or send your email:

www.Favorintl.org
info@favorintl.org

You can also mail your tax-deductible donation to:
Favor International Inc.
1767 Lakewood Ranch Rd. #223
Bradenton, FL 34211

Another way to help is by inviting Carole to speak at your church, organization or conference during the times she visits the U.S.

The phone number to schedule your event is:
941-444-9940

Please, feel free to check out how to get the newsletters and other information about the ministry to find out what the needs are and the many wonderful things God is doing in more detail on our upcoming new website.

One more favor. If you liked this book, please write a review on Amazon. Your encouraging words help with sales and that helps the ministry.